PRACTISING THE PRINCIPLES OF PRAYER

PRACTISING
the
PRINCIPLES
of
PRAYER

David Pawson

Terra Nova Publications

Published in Great Britain by
Terra Nova Publications International Ltd.
Orders and enquiries: PO Box 2400 Bradford on Avon BA15 2YN
Registered Office (not for trade): 21 St. Thomas Street, Bristol BS1 6JS

Extracts from The Book of Common Prayer, the rights in which are
vested in the Crown, are reproduced by permission of the Crown's
Patentee, Cambridge University Press.

Cover design by Roger Judd

ISBN 978 1 901949 58 2

Printed in Great Britain by
Creative Print and Design Group, Blaina

PREFACE

This book is based on a series of talks. Originating as it does from the spoken word, its style will be found by many readers to be somewhat different from my usual written style. It is hoped that this will not detract from the substance of the biblical teaching found here.

As always, I ask the reader to compare everything I say or write with what is written in the Bible and, if at any point a conflict is found, always to rely upon the clear teaching of Scripture.

David Pawson

Contents

1

PRAYER TO THE FATHER

I am fed up with those who tell us that we are just animals. It is no wonder that people behave as if they are in the jungle when they are told this so often. You may remember that in his books *The Naked Ape* and *The Human Zoo*, zoologist Desmond Morris tried to see animal feelings and behaviour in human beings. The late Johnny Morris, fellow zoologist and television presenter, did it in a more subtle way, trying to show human feelings and thoughts in animals. Both of them brought the animal and the human world far too close, for the Bible makes it clear that we are not animals. We may breathe the same air, we may have a similar digestive system, but we are different. If you tell a man that he is an animal you must expect him to behave that way. But I think it is an insult to the animal world; we are more barbaric to each other in the human race than animals have ever been known to be. We can sink to depths that no animal can sink to, and we can rise to heights to which no animal can rise.

Philosophers have debated the difference between animals and men for many years. Some have said that only men make tools, but since a girl went to live among a colony of chimpanzees in Africa – a Christian girl, by the way, who took a Bible with her – she discovered that they made tools, so that difference has disappeared from the anthropology books. Others have said, 'Well, humans laugh.' I suppose the hyena does in a way, but I do not think that is the difference. Others say, 'Well, human beings talk to each other', but we are finding out more and more about animal communication, and even how fish communicate with each other. Some have said that man's uniqueness lies in the fact that he cooks, and certainly the animals have not discovered or used fire yet. But I believe the one basic difference between all the animals in the world and your writer here is that man *prays*. Not even Snoopy ever relates to the powers beyond! Charlie Brown and Lucy may sit and ask questions about the stars, but Snoopy never does. And even though a lot of human thoughts and feelings are put into that dog's mind and heart, nevertheless Schultz, who was a Sunday school teacher for a number of years and, alas, became an agnostic – which was reflected in Peanuts cartoons – never dared to put religious thoughts into Snoopy's mind, because that would have been too grotesque to be believable. I can talk to my dog about this world. I can talk about walks and bones and scrapings and other things and she can understand, but I cannot pray with my dog. She has never shown any desire whatsoever to do so!

Praying, this unique activity of the human race, was there back at the beginning. As far back as we can dig into the history of our race, we find that in the earliest days the simplest, most primitive human beings believed in a great power, a great God who lived above the sky, to whom you could speak. When I went to New Zealand, I was very struck with the spiritism still among the Maori. I am afraid it made me shiver. I felt insulted when the New Zealand airline presented me with a green plastic idol (Tikki) — that in our technological age I should be given that for 'good luck' as I flew in. I am sorry, I do not intend any insult to your country if you are a Maori; we do the same here. The Maori have gods of the sky, the sea, the rivers and mountains. But I was fascinated to read that when they first came to New Zealand, a thousand years ago, they believed in one God only, and he was the God who lived above the sky called *Yah*, which is the first part of the word *Yahweh*, which is God's name.

You find the same among the Aborigines of Australia. You find the same among the pygmies. And anthropologists have discovered that the worship of things on earth is a later addition, a corruption of man's early knowledge that there was one God above the sky — a power beyond the stars to whom you could relate, to whom you could talk.

So down through the ages men have prayed; it is almost an instinctive thing. I suppose that the majority of people – certainly in this land and,

I think I am fair in saying, throughout the world – pray at some time or another. They know that the human race is unable to solve its own problems. They reach out, in however vague and misty a way, and they pray.

So we pray, and it is an instinctive thing. Yet I am going to be writing about Christian prayer, which is not instinctive but distinctive. It is not the same thing for a Christian to be praying as for a Tibetan monk to be revolving his prayer wheel, or a Muslim with his mat out facing Mecca. There are profound differences in prayer, and Christian prayer is unique. The rest is instinctive and spreads right through the human race, taking many forms, but Christian prayer is distinctive and I want to tell you what is distinctive about it.

First, for many in this world prayer is a private thing. For the Christian, though, prayer can never be private. There is an important sense in which a Christian can never pray alone! If you compare this with Islam (which is seeking to spread its teaching in Britain), you find that in that faith one can pray alone. Muslims believe that Mohammed is Allah's prophet, but you do not even need Mohammed

— a Muslim alone with Allah can pray. Now a Christian can never do that. The very minimum for a Christian to pray is four persons present, and it is very rarely that you can pray without that absolute minimum. The minimum of four persons is: you, the Father, the Son and the Spirit. You pray to the Father, through the Son and in the Spirit, or it is not Christian prayer at all, which is why I say that at least four of you are involved and a Christian can never pray alone.

Furthermore, as soon as you get on your knees the devil is involved and interested. That is one of the reasons why prayer is such a battle and such a problem — so that makes five of you! You then discover that the devil never comes alone. When you pray you will find, if you really get through to the heavenly places, that there are a lot of others joining in, and you will be wrestling not against flesh and blood but against principalities and powers in the heavenly places. That sentence in Ephesians chapter 6 comes in the context of praying. So they are going to be involved. There is safety in numbers, and there are many special promises in Scripture to Christians that if two or three of you

agree on earth – that is, touching anything – then
your praye

So there
to one, in
religion, bu
it is always
into the fr
you are sur
you are wr
you are pra
in the Spir
minions ar
too, over one sinner who is repenting, and prayer
is a very public occasion.

In this book I am going to be offering some
practical tips, to try to help you. Have you ever
noticed that, when Jesus taught you how to pray
'privately', he said: "Go into a room, shut the door
and say, 'OUR Father' . . . ."? Not 'my Father' —he
was the only one who used that phrase. When you
pray alone you are to shut the door and say give
us our daily bread. He was saying as clearly as he
could there is no such thing as private prayer. It
is always public, always part of a family, always

part of a crowd. In fact, whatever need you have, others in God's family have that same need at that point and you can pray for them with yourself. That is why on a number of occasions when I have taken a funeral, in the first prayer I have prayed – and led the mourners to pray – I have mentioned other funerals taking place at that time and other people mourning, because there are others, and in a funeral you can be preoccupied with your own grief.

There is another difference, too. For many in the world prayer is meditation, but for Christians it is not meditation it is conversation. I must explain this very clearly, because the concept of prayer as meditation, as a higher form of prayer, has crept in within Christian circles. It has been around for centuries. It came in originally from Eastern mysticism and it is not biblical prayer. The idea is this: that if you are still at the stage of simply asking for things and talking to God you are in the 'primary department' of prayer, and that once you have stopped talking and asking for things and have learned just to think about things you have moved up a stage in prayer to meditation, and that you can even move on from that — and those who espouse transcendental meditation would say move on from that to thinking about nothing, and then you are really there!

It is not just coming in the form of transcendental meditation. There is a Christian mysticism that has got it upside down and thinks that talking to God and asking him for things is a very low form of prayer. Let me ask you to do a little biblical checking. Go through everything Jesus said about prayer, and 95% of it is about talking and about asking—95% of it! To Jesus, prayer was talking and asking, not thinking. There is a place for meditation in the Christian life, which is to meditate in God's Word—not to think of nothing and see what comes into your mind, but to meditate in God's law day and night. Though there is a place for meditation, it is meditation with content, and that is not prayer. Prayer is talking to God and asking him for things, if the teaching of Jesus is anything to go by, and that is the highest form of prayer, not the lowest.

Furthermore, if you have studied Jesus' own prayer life you will find that the same holds true. Study his prayer in Gethsemane, study John 17, which is the fullest prayer of Jesus we have, and count up how many things he asks for. He is not meditating, he is talking and he is asking, all the way through. That then is the heart of Christian prayer. So let us realise, simple though it is, that talking to God about our needs and his desires is prayer. When the disciples said, 'Lord, teach us to pray', he did not give them a meditational system, he gave them a simple form of words to say out loud, not to think; he did not say, 'When you pray, think', he said, 'When you pray, say . . . .' Then he told them six things, and every one of them was *asking*. There were three things that God wanted them to ask for, and three things that they would want to ask for themselves, but it was speaking and it was asking, and that was prayer. Now this is so profound yet so simple. I point it out because even Christians get lost in mystical meditation and think they have got into a higher form of prayer. Prayer is simple. It is a child telling his Father what he needs. That is the heart of it.

I can go a little further and say I do not find scriptural warrant for thinking that you have had a better time together if it has all been praise and there has been no asking. God likes prayer and praise and he does not value them over and against each other. Yet we can sometimes think that if we have had a time of praise and not asked for anything that God must somehow be more pleased than if we had brought a shopping list —but he is a Father who loves us to express our needs, and Jesus said, 'Go and tell him what you need', and that is what he wants to hear.

There was a famous violinist and his own son learned the violin, but not from his father, he learned from another violinist who was not nearly as good as his father. And someone said to the father, 'Why didn't you teach him?' And the violinist said, 'Because he never asked me.' He never asked. That father was just waiting for the boy to say, 'Please would you teach me.' That is what God is waiting for, people just to say 'please'. They can praise him when the answers come. But study our Lord's teaching on prayer and it is speaking and asking.

Here is tip number two. You will find it very much easier when you are 'alone' to pray if you pray out loud. Are you troubled by wandering thoughts?

Then try words. Words do not wander as thoughts do. It is such an obvious thing to say, but try it. One of the reasons why many Christians find it difficult to pray out loud in a prayer meeting is because they have never prayed out loud privately. They have never got used to the sound of their own voice. So they have a double psychological barrier to get over in praying in front of others: they have not only got to pray in front of others, they have got to pray in front of themselves. *'When you want to pray,'* said Jesus, *'go into a room, shut the door, and say . . . .'* How simple! How did we miss it? Yet the majority of Christians I counsel and speak to in this country *think* their prayers, which is a very difficult thing to do – much harder than just to say them – and Jesus said, "*Say*, 'our Father . . . .'" I am trying to keep this simple. You may think I am being a bit obvious, even quibbling, but I want to be helpful and practical —and if you are way past all this, then God bless you, I will try and catch up with you some day, but I want to start where people are.

As soon as you mention the subject of prayer people say, 'I wonder if he is going to deal with the problems of prayer.' Now I want to begin with the privileges of prayer. If you begin with the problems you are finished. My wife and I read certain books before our marriage and they were very helpful, but we got to a point where we had read too much. We thought, how many things can go wrong! We were reading too much about the problems. You can get worried about the problems, so we began to think of the privilege. I want you to concentrate on the privilege rather than the problems. There are problems, there are difficulties, and we will mention them as we go along, but let us start with the privilege, the sheer honour it is to be able to pray.

Some time ago I was standing on the kerbside on a street in London when a beautiful maroon Rolls Royce drew up at the traffic lights, just a yard from me. I looked at the car first, and then I thought I would see who was inside. And there, about a yard from me, was Her Majesty The Queen! And I have never been quite so embarrassed. I did not know quite what to do. She sort of looked at me and I sort of waved my hand, and she sort of responded. But there was plate glass between us, and that was as near as we got, then she sailed on. Supposing she had wound down the window and said, 'Hello', and supposing she had said, 'Here is my card, drop in and see me some time', and supposing she had said, 'Here is my card, if there is anything you want just get on the blower' —no, she would not have talked like that, would she! Well, you might laugh, but I can tell you this: a hot line to Buckingham Palace which you can use at any time is nothing compared to the privilege of prayer, for the Queen does not have a millionth of the resources that God has. That is the privilege of prayer. It is not a problem. We start here: we have a hot line. I sometimes find myself amazed at just assuming that I can simply close my eyes, or even keep them open, and say, 'God' —and I am through to him. If he just provided me one interview in a lifetime, that would be a privilege, would it not? Just one!

It is not a question of mastering the mechanics so much as practising the presence. Many people are looking for a method of prayer, and that is what develops a ritual, it does not develop a relationship. And, greatly daring, I will say that the Bible has nothing to say about what we tend to call a 'quiet

time'. It says *pray at all times*, it does not say have
a quiet time. Now I want you to think through the
implications of that. I want you to imagine me as
a husband saying to my wife, 'I'm going to love
you every Wednesday and Friday evening prompt
at nine-thirty, and you can have a whole half hour
of my time and I'll set the alarm clock. How about
that?' Is that a relationship? I believe that it is
not so much a matter of mastering the mechanics
or having a method as *practising the presence*. Of
course I am quoting there Brother Lawrence, who
in his kitchen practised the presence of God, so
that as he scrubbed pots and pans it was natural to
talk to his Father and to ask for what he needed.

So prayer is a privilege rather than a problem,
and if you really want to do a thing you will find a
way. If a young man looks around in church and
sees a young lady he rather fancies, he will find a
way. He will form his own mechanics: he will send
her a letter or he will just be around in the foyer
afterwards, or he will send her a valentine next
February; he will do *something*. It is the person who
matters, more than the place or anything else, and
the Master matters more than the method.

For many, prayer is 'fortune', but for Christians it is faith. I mean by 'fortune' that for many people prayer is like a game of chance or 'luck', as if God is a kind of heavenly game show host with a big barrel, and we all send our prayers up and he puts them in the big barrel and turns the handle, opens it up, and now and again he pulls out your name and address and gives you an answer. People who have sent up many prayers and got just one or two answers back seem to think it is a matter of luck that it seems to come up —about as often as a premium bond is likely to. Lest you think I am lampooning, let me describe something I received through the post. It was headed 'Think Prayer', and underneath that it said, 'Trust in the Lord with all your heart and he will light your way', followed by this:

'This prayer has been sent to you for good luck. It originally came from the Netherlands. (Sorry, friends, but that is where it came from!) It has been around the world nine times. The luck has been sent to you. You are to receive good luck within four days after receiving this copy. This is no joke, you will receive it in the mail. Send twenty copies of this letter to friends you think need good luck. Please do not send money. Do not keep this letter. It must leave within 96 hours after receiving it. A United States officer received $7000, one man received $60,000 but lost it because he broke the chain.' (Well, hard luck!) 'Now the more serious side. While in the Philippines General W' (whoever he is) 'lost his life six days after receiving this copy and failing to circulate this prayer. However, before his death he received $775,000 which he had won, and which he had to leave behind.'

Needless to say, you should never pay any attention whatsoever to such nonsensical letters! 'I shot an arrow into the air; it fell to earth I know not where!' The point is that many people do feel about asking God for things that it is 'chancy'; that it is 'worth trying', that it 'might work'. But for Christians prayer is not fortune — prayer is *faith*. There is a certainty. If there is one principle that takes the 'luck' out of prayer, takes the 'chance' out of it, it is the principle which we must now look at — the principle of faith. Although there are other principles which will qualify this I am going to concentrate on faith.

Jesus said, *Have faith in God*. Or, to give you the flavour of the Greek, *Go on having faith in God*. It is not a once and for all thing that you did at the day of your conversion. *Go on* having faith in God. That is the foundation of prayer, and it must be there before prayer can be more than a 'chancy business'.

Some people may assume that what I mean by that phrase is that I must believe that what I ask I will receive. That is only the seventh thing that is involved in my mind in the phrase 'Have faith in God'. There are six things that you must believe first, before you can believe that you will get your answer.

Here, then, are seven things which make up faith in God, which gets answers to prayer.

1. I MUST BELIEVE THAT GOD IS THERE.

Have you noticed this in Hebrews 11? Whoever would come to God must believe that he exists. That is the first item in faith, if I am going to pray in faith. I must believe that God is there. The atheist says he is not there; the agnostic does not know. The atheist does not pray at all. The agnostic does when he is in a jam, but he does not know if the prayer is going to be answered. The Christian says, 'I believe that God is there.' Talking to yourself is of no use. Some people think that a period of auto-suggestive meditation is helpful each day, but I am not keen to talk to myself. For one thing, I do not like listening to what I have got to say. I am not a very good conversationalist with myself. And if you do too much talking to yourself that is the first step on a slippery slope, mentally speaking! If prayer is just talking to myself, then I am not going to do it. I must believe that God is there to talk to. That is step number one.

The first problem is that my physical faculties cannot tell me that God is there. I have no problem talking to someone I can see, or whose arm I can grasp, or even somebody I can smell who is there. But in prayer you are talking to someone you cannot see and someone you cannot hear, hold or touch, whom you cannot smell and you cannot taste —and therefore it feels a bit unreal.

My mental faculties cannot tell me that he is there either, because the great philosophers of the world have failed to agree on whether there is a God or not. They have used every ounce of intellect they have. They have deduced, they have argued logically, and still they cannot tell me whether or not God exists. So neither my physical nor my mental faculties can tell me, therefore I am driven back to a spiritual faculty — faith. That is the only faculty that can tell me he is there. Did you notice that I did not write *feeling*? One of the basic problems of faith is expressed in this statement, which so many people have uttered: 'I don't *feel* that he is there.' You show me in the Bible where it says you need to! It only says you have to have faith that he is there. Sometimes you will feel him so close that you almost feel you could touch him, but at other times you will not. The Bible is indifferent as to whether you feel his presence or not. It poses the question, 'Do you have faith that he is there?' *Not feeling*. It is not, 'Whoever would pray must *feel* that he exists'! His word is enough, and he always keeps his word. So by faith, whether I feel like it or not, I can say, 'Our Father, you are in heaven. You are there.'

2. I MUST BELIEVE NOT ONLY THAT GOD EXISTS BUT THAT HE IS PERSONAL, THAT HE IS SOME*ONE* NOT SOME*THING*.

There are many colloquial synonyms for God, phrases that people use. Some years ago, a Bishop of Woolwich popularised one in his book *Honest to God*, calling God 'the ground of our being'. I would find it rather difficult to talk to 'the ground of my being'. Others talk of 'the life force'. It is not easy to talk to a force. You might as well pray to an electric socket in the wall. There is power there! But it is a thing, not a person. Before I pray, I must believe not only that God is there, but that he is someone, not something. Most people say, 'Well, there is something greater than the universe, there is some power out there.' But it is not a power you pray to. God, to whom you pray, is personal. Prayer is unreal if you only try to talk to a power. That bishop admitted that since he believed in God as the ground of his being his prayer life had been shot to pieces, because he did not know who to pray to. He was holding a conversation with the ground of his own being — in other words, he was talking to himself.

29

A student at the College of Law in Guildford, to whom I was talking about this very matter, said, 'God? That is only a name for my religious feelings' —and he meant it.

I replied, 'Well, you can't pray to your own religious feelings.'

'No, I can't. I don't,' he said.

So we believe God is personal. Why? Because the Bible tells me that I am made in the image of God, and I feel, I think and I act. God feels, thinks and acts. I am personal and he is personal.

I am not making God in my own image; I am made in his. But in an important sense we are 'like' each other —and you can talk to people you are like. I have heard people say, 'I just couldn't keep up a conversation with that person, they are so different from me in outlook, in temperament, in background. I couldn't talk to them freely, they are just so unlike me.' But, praise God, by faith, I can believe that God is in this sense 'like' me. Of course there are many other senses in which he is unlike me, but the point is that I can know him because he is personal, not impersonal. That requires a big step of faith. He is not *just* a person. Notice that

I did not write of believing that God *is a person*, but to believe that *he is personal* —which means something more than that he is a person, because he is more. He is three persons, and he has always known how to communicate as three persons because he is three persons communicating.

Now this, to me, is the most exciting difference between Allah and Jehovah, the Father of our Lord Jesus. The god of Islam is only one, therefore he is not love. He cannot be, because no one person by himself can be love. Therefore the statement 'God is love' does not appear in the Koran, it appears in the Bible. If Allah is god, then there was a period in time when he was all by himself, and there was nobody else. So how could Allah love? Do you understand what I am saying? God is personal. Father has been talking with Son, and Son with Father, from all eternity, so he is personal, and I can get in on the conversation; I can break in, because I am made in his image and I can communicate, and I can talk. He communicates; he is love. It is as if the three of them, the three of him – I do not quite know how to put this, it is almost too wonderful for words – are opening their arms and saying communicate with us, we are personal—and talked together about it before they made us.

3. I MUST TAKE A STEP OF FAITH THAT GOD CAN HEAR.

When I preach in church I use amplification so that the whole congregation can hear. And I can pick up a telephone and be heard over a much greater distance. When I was in New Zealand I got through to my wife back in England in seconds, and we talked via satellites out in space with no discernible lag between question and answer — marvellous! People on earth talked to a man on the moon with only a slightly discernible time lag. We are getting further and further out, but I tell you this, from the very beginning a man who prayed could be heard in highest heaven. It takes big faith to believe that God can hear each of us out of the millions of voices. There are two problems. There is the problem of distance: how far away is God? He is in highest heaven. Where is that? I do not have a clue. I just know that my voice reaches highest heaven! But there is a problem of numbers, too. Have you ever been in a room where so many people are talking that you cannot hear what is being said? If you are one of those who has to wear a hearing aid then you will understand, because many hearing aids cannot direct themselves, and pick up every cough, every noise, every voice; it is very difficult to pick out the one person you are trying to listen to. And I just wonder how many people God is listening to at this very minute. Yet he hears every word. There are over six thousand million of us on the earth, and he hears every word that is spoken.

He knows every word, even before I utter it. He knows when I get out of a chair, he knows when I sit down, and he hears every word. He is hearing every word at this very minute in highest heaven. It takes faith to believe this, but it is true. Such knowledge is too wonderful for me; it is high, and I cannot attain to that. I cannot listen to more than one person at once, but God is God.

This brings me to the next thing: the faith that he will listen. There is a difference between being able to hear and actually listening. Sometimes I am told that I am a bad listener, and I know that is true. I have no trouble with hearing, but I sometimes have trouble with my listening. However, faith says not only that God can hear my prayer but that he will listen to it.

The extraordinary thing is that we think we have a right to be heard. We consider that we have a right to live, a right to health, a right to happiness —so we think we have a right to demand these things from God, as if he is a 'welfare state' for us! What right have we to be heard? What right have I to demand a listening ear from God? People have said to me, 'Well, I didn't ask to be put in this world; I didn't create myself; God put me here, so I have a right to ask for health and happiness from him.' You have no such right, and I will tell you why, very simply. It is because when God made this world and made us, he said, 'That is very good, now keep it that way' —and not one of us has done so. Therefore, we have forfeited the right to be listened to. We have no right. God, in mercy, listens. By faith you can believe that God will not only hear what you say but that he will listen.

Do you realise how many barriers there could be between you and God? If only one sin in your life has been committed by you each day over the last thirty years, there are now ten thousand sins between you and God! What right have you to be heard? Only if your sins are dealt with have you the right to be heard —and yet God listens; he loves to listen, not because of what I am but because of what he is. Because he is a person of such love that he loves to listen. He loves us to tell him of our needs.

Next, I must believe not only that God will listen but that he will reply. Conversation can be miserable if it is one-sided, can it not? Think of what it is like if you have to do all the talking: 'Nice weather we're having. Nice weather yesterday, wasn't it? Hope it will be nice weather tomorrow . . . .' It is a one-way conversation and you are having to keep it up. Prayer with God is more conversation than meditation, and conversation is a two-way thing. To believe that God will reply is part of the faith that is needed. Have faith in God — that he exists, that he is personal, that he can hear, that he will listen, that he can reply, that he has a mouth as well as ears. It is important when we pray not to tell God how he must reply.

Here again is a practical tip. If you lay down

beforehand how he must reply, then you are likely to miss his reply. And he changes his methods of reply. There are many — I can list only a few. First, he can reply by vibrating the air so that your physical ear can hear his voice. He really can, but when he does it sounds like a clap of thunder and I am grateful that he does not reply that way too often! God can make the air move. We know that when he speaks it sounds like thunder, because on a number of occasions in the Bible when he spoke, people said that was what it sounded like. Some caught the words, 'This is my beloved Son in whom I am well pleased.' Those who like quiet, dignified worship would certainly not come near church if God spoke every time like that!

He can speak to us through our reading the Bible. There are times when a verse seems to leap out, as if it is written in shining letters with your name and address on it. But how fatal if he has spoken to you in that way on one occasion to try to get the answer that same way the next time.

He can speak to you through an inner voice which is so clear that you can even think that you heard it with your ears. Sometimes, when going out of the church building, people have said to me, 'You know, when you said that, it was God's word to me.' Now I can remember everything I have said in a sermon immediately afterwards, and I know that I have not said that, yet they were convinced that I did. It was actually God who had spoken so clearly within their heart that they heard him, and they thought I said it because when they were listening to me they were open to listening to him.

He can speak through circumstances astonishingly. He can speak through another human voice, either through an immediate word of prophecy or through a casual remark in a conversation. The important thing is not how he answers, or even when he answers, it is to believe that when you pray he will reply. Sometimes he does not reply until the last minute, but faith believes that he will reply in time, it does not dictate how or when that reply should come.

Sometimes an answer comes immediately. If I think back over my life to certain crucial steps which led me to become a preacher, I can see a great variety of ways in which God spoke. When I thought of going into the ministry, I said one morning, 'Lord, you must tell me before midday today if you want me in the ministry.'

I had coffee at about eleven o'clock with my friend – we were both training to be farmers – and he looked at me and said, 'You know, David,' and this was right out of the blue, 'I think you are going to finish up in a pulpit and not behind a plough.'

So I left him and I went out into the street, where I bumped right into a retired minister, who looked straight at me and he too, out of the blue, said, 'David, when are you going to get into the ministry?' Now here was God speaking through other people, as clearly as you could ask, before noon that day.

I think of when the time came for me to face the fact that I was a heretic in the denomination in which I was a minister – as far as the matter of baptism went – and had to appear before a doctrinal committee made up of theologians of that denomination, and I did not relish the prospect at all. About two weeks before that, I was on holiday in a little fishing village on the coast of Northumberland, and a dear fisherman got up in the pulpit and read God's word from Hebrews: *I will not fear what man shall do to me*. As he spoke, all fear left. Although we lost job, home, pension, everything, God had spoken; his word came alive and the fear went.

Then I think of the next voice I heard through circumstances, when Gold Hill Baptist Church said, 'We are calling you to be the pastor; will you come?'

I said, 'I'm sorry, but I can't come until next April 30th at the earliest.' It was then November.

They said, 'Isn't that strange? We are building a new manse, and the builder told us that it would be finished on April 30th.' It was, and we moved in on April 30th. Circumstances!

Then I think of our move to Guildford, and how twice the church wrote and said, 'Will you come to Guildford to be pastor?' I wrote back and said, 'nothing doing', or words to that effect! But one morning, as I was in bed, not feeling very well that day, there up on the wallpaper was the word 'Guildford'. I said, 'Lord, should I not have said no?' My wife brought in the breakfast tray. There was the mail on a plate, and the top envelope had a Guildford postmark. She will remember my turning to her after reading the letter and saying,

'We're going to Guildford.' We look back and see that God speaks in a thousand and one ways. The important thing is to believe that he is going to reply, not to tell him how or when. I hope this is practical enough for you!

It is vital to believe that God can act, that he is a living God, in living control of the situation, and that prayer changes things, not just people. Now I am going to give you a little philosophy lesson. There are three philosophies to consider here: theism, deism and monism. Theists say that God created and controls this universe. Deists say that God created this universe but he cannot control it; it is like a watch that he made and wound up, and it now controls itself. Monists say that this world created itself and controls itself. Monism does not allow for prayer at all, but deism is far too common inside the church. Deists say you can pray about people because God can change people, but you cannot pray about things because God is no longer in control of them. For example, you cannot pray about the weather, for that is controlled by natural laws. You can pray about yourself, and pray for patience for yourself, and you can pray about the sick. A theist says that God not only created, he controls.

I was listening to Mendelssohn's *Elijah*, that matchless oratorio, which I had previously listened to out at Ein Gev on the Sea of Galilee on an Easter Sunday evening. I thought of Elijah as I looked out at the garden, and seeing how dry it was I thought, 'I wonder if a prophet in Britain would dare to say, "God, stop the rain for three and a half years until we come to our senses."' After just a few months of light rainfall we begin to get worried! By prayer, that righteous man stopped the rain for three and a half years. Imagine what would occur in Britain if that happened! We are far more likely to be on our knees quickly begging for rain as soon as the tap runs dry. But Elijah had seen the real need of the people when he said, 'God, stop that rain for three and a half years.'

I remember being in the hot desert wind and feeling how it dried everything up, and reflected on what that would have been like for three and a half years. And when I was on Mount Carmel at the very spot where Elijah challenged the prophets of Baal, I took a photograph of a cloud the size of a man's hand, right above me. Elijah believed that God can control, that he can act —that he is a living God.

Watchman Nee did this, too. He and a young boy went to evangelise an island off mainland China, and when they got there they found a fertility cult that worshipped a god which the people believed sent the rain. There was an annual procession of this idol, when it was carried down the street by the priest. This took place in dry weather; the local people walked along in the sun, and they asked that god to bring the rain a few weeks later, and the rain came. The pair tried preaching the gospel, but nothing happened. As they prayed about it, this fourteen year-old boy said to Watchman Nee, 'Why don't we do an "Elijah" on them?'

Watchman Nee's faith was not quite up to it, but he said, 'Okay, let's.' And they prayed that on the day the people brought the idol out that it would rain on the idol. All through the coming weeks, the sky remained cloudless and blue. When they got up on the morning of the procession, the sky was still cloudless and blue, and their faith shook a little. Then the procession down the street with the idol began, and a cloud started to form. It spread quickly, and the first drops came. It poured with rain, the priest carrying the idol slipped — and it smashed! The priests hurriedly stuck it together and announced publicly that they had made a mistake about the date, and that they would bring the god out some weeks later.

Watchman Nee said, 'It will not rain until that day you bring it again, and then it will rain again.' It did, and the island turned to the Lord. You see, you have to believe that God is still in control, that he can act, and he can change things, not just people.

We were going to have our first Easter Sunday sunrise service in Guildford. We met for our Saturday morning prayer meeting, depressed because the weather forecast was bad. It was the first sunrise service in our town, as far as we knew, and we felt it was for the glory of the Lord. We prayed, 'Lord, you are our "weather man".' We prayed for his glory, not for the sake of our service or for our organisation — this was different from praying for a nice day for your Sunday school outing. We prayed for his glory, for the first service. That Sunday morning we saw record sunshine — the best in Guildford for sixteen years. Should we dismiss it as a coincidence? You are welcome to, but I would rather live in a series of such 'coincidences' — and that requires faith that God is in control, that he has not simply made the world and then left it to run on natural laws. The natural laws are to God what the school rules are to the headmaster. He can change them any time he wants to do so.

The last thing that we need to believe is this: God will give us what we ask for. Now you might have thought that I would have mentioned this first when writing about praying in faith. But I mention it last. All these other things need to be believed first: that God really is there; that he is personal; that he can hear; that he will listen; that he can reply; that he can act. Then, if I am sure of those six things, I can pray, in faith, that I will have what I ask for. It is that kind of faith that gets answers. Jesus said, *'Therefore I tell you, whatever you ask in prayer believe that you have it and you will.'* That is an extremely strong statement. His brother James, writing many years later, said, *But when you ask, don't doubt, like a wave being tossed in the sea.* Don't doubt. This is the problem: doubts come in; worry comes in. Will it happen? Will it be alright? As Jesus taught us, worry is a libel on your heavenly Father. *'O you of little faith.'*

There are so many stories, it is hard to know where to begin. I think of that Lincolnshire ploughboy John Hunt, who taught himself to read his Bible by balancing it on his plough handles while he ploughed the fields. He taught himself Greek and Hebrew the same way. He went out at the age of twenty-six to Tonga and Fiji as the first missionary, and that led to those islands turning to Christ within ten years; and then he died at thirty-six, worn out with his labours. On the outward voyage the ship came within sight of Fiji when it was wrecked on a coral reef and was breaking up beneath his feet. It looked as if that journey had been for nothing, and they would all be drowned — there was no hope. But John Hunt got down on his knees on the deck and said, 'Lord, we've come to bring your gospel. Get us there.' When he opened his eyes, to his horror he saw a great tidal wave bearing down on them — the wave having started in an underwater volcano way out in the Pacific. Instead of drowning them, though, it lifted what remained of the ship, carried it a mile, and dropped it on the shore. Every man walked off it. He believed!

I sometimes get a bit depressed by reading books on answers to prayer. Do you? You read the life of George Müller and Hudson Taylor, and you just want to crawl away and give up. There are two things not to do with your faith, and two things to do with it. Let us be practical. Here are the things not to do with it. Do not try and *feel* your faith. Your feelings go up and down; if they did not do so, you would not have any. But if you tie your faith to your feelings, your faith will go up and down too. Tie your feelings to your faith, then your feelings will follow your faith. Tie your faith to the facts. That is the right way round. Nor must you try to force your faith. You can read the life of George Müller and then try to force yourself to open a big orphanage! Forcing faith does not work. What do you do to your faith? First, you stimulate it, then you stretch it. Stimulate your faith by listening to other answers to prayer.

There was a young teenage boy from my congregation, on a school outing, who had a small
problem. While travelling on the coach he wanted
to eat the orange that had been given him with his
packed lunch. The problem was what to do with
the orange peel. The ashtrays were all jammed
full and he did not want to put it in his pocket. So
what did he do? He prayed, in faith, asking God to
deal with the problem. Another boy tapped him on
the shoulder and asked him, 'What are you going
to do with that peel?'

'Why do you ask?' he replied.

'Well,' the other boy said, 'I like eating it. Can I
have it?'

The boy who had prayed deliberately went
around the bus and asked, 'Do you eat orange peel?'
And he got a resounding 'no' from every other
boy. It is amusing, but to me it is tremendously
encouraging, because he just asked about a simple
problem, and the Lord heard, and the Lord put
it right. That is all of a piece with the Lord who
turned water into wine when they got into a little
embarrassment at a wedding reception at Cana of
Galilee.

Stimulate your faith by listening to answers to prayer, and stimulate your faith by reading the Bible. As you get into the Bible you live in a world in which people talk to God and he talks to them. You live in a real world; it is fact, not fiction; it is not a science text book, but it is not myth either. It is a world in which real people brought their real needs to God, asked him about them, and had them met. The more you read your Bible, the more you live in that kind of world, and the more you will do what the people in the Bible did.

Stimulate your faith; do not try to feel it, do not try and force it, but stimulate it, and stretch it from within. I learned this message from a French missionary. He said to me, 'David, never pray outside your faith', and I thought: 'What on earth does he mean by that?'

'God is able to do exceedingly more than we ask or even imagine. That is what Paul says in Ephesians chapter 3. Do you know the hymn *Therefore thou art coming to a King, large petitions with thee bring*?'

I said to the missionary, 'What do you mean? He is able to do anything.'

He replied, 'Yes, he is able to, and he often will do more than you ask or imagine, but you must learn to pray within your faith.'

He continued, 'I learned this lesson with my next door neighbour. When they moved in, I put them on my prayer list and was praying for them daily – for their conversion – and nothing happened. Finally, I said to the Lord, "Why? You're not showing me any answer to my prayer. I'm praying daily for my neighbour." The Lord said, "Because you don't believe it." I replied, "But Lord, you can do anything,"' The Lord said, "I know I can, but you don't believe it."'

He said, 'But I do, Lord, anything is possible for you', and the Lord said, 'No you don't, you can't imagine your neighbour as a Christian, can you?' He replied, 'No, I can't!' So he asked what he should pray for, and the Lord said, 'Pray for something that you can believe will happen.' So then he prayed that he might have a good conversation with his neighbour. And within a week they had had a great talk over the garden fence. So then he prayed that he might get into the house next door, something which he had never done. Shortly after that, his neighbour asked him in for coffee. Then he prayed that the neighbour would bring the subject round to religion, and the neighbour asked him where he went on Sundays. Then he prayed that he might get the neighbour along to something at church, and the neighbour came.

Do you see what he was doing? He was stretching his faith from the inside. He was praying within his faith, and as he stretched it from the inside, it was growing. Until, finally, he said, 'Lord, convert my neighbour' —and he was converted.

So do not try to feel your faith; do not try to force it; but stimulate it by studying answers to prayer, particularly in the Bible, and stretch it from inside by praying within your faith. It is much better to pray for something small that you can believe, so that when God replies to your faith it will grow that little bit, and you will pray for something more.

Often one listens to prayers such as, 'Lord, send revival to our town!' I want to stop that person and say: 'What is in your mind when you pray that prayer? What do you think will happen? And can you see that happening? Would it not be better to start with something you could believe would happen, that you can see happening with the eye of faith even though it is invisible to you as yet?' Start within your faith and stretch it from inside.

Let us now look at the objective side of faith. The objective side is Fatherhood. Faith has to have content; it has to be 'faith in . . .' and my faith meets his Fatherhood. For what is peculiar to Christian prayer – which you will find nowhere else in the world, in no other religion, in no book of another religion – is this. One day the disciples heard Jesus praying. Now they were men who had been brought up to say their prayers, they were men who knew *what* to say, but when they listened to Jesus pray, that was something different. When he had finished, they crowded round and said, 'Lord, teach us to pray.' They did not say 'Lord, teach us *how* to pray' — they were not asking for a method. They were saying: Lord, could you teach us to talk to God like you do? Could you teach us to pray? And he said yes, I can. *'When you pray, say, "Abba" . . . .'* For a Jew that is a revolution. For anyone, it may seem incredible. You go to all the people who do not come to church, and who say they believe in God, and count how many times they use the word 'Father' about him —not once. 'Oh, I believe in God', they say. 'I don't want you to think I don't believe in God.' But they don't say 'Father', do they? Of course they don't, because they are not his children.

Even in the Jewish religion, which came nearer to the truth than any other, which prepared for the truth and was the foundation for it, they were so afraid of taking God's name in vain that even to this day they will not pronounce it. In Israel I asked a Jewish man about this. I tried to push him hard on it, but as hard as I pushed him I could not get him to do it. I was trying to be sensitive in every other area, but I pushed him on this, saying, 'I never know, when I am preaching, how to pronounce the name of God; would you tell me?' He was giving me a Hebrew lesson, and he told me I should say 'Eliahu' and 'Moishe', and I shouldn't say 'Jesus', I should say 'Yeshua', and not 'Messiah' but 'Meshiah', and 'Izra', not 'Ezra'. I said, 'Right, now how do I pronounce the name of God?' He looked as if I had slapped him in the face and then said, 'I'll tell you the letters.' So he told me the four letters, which I knew anyway. I asked, 'Now how do I say those?' He said, 'Jews don't say it.' I said, 'Well, if they did say it, how would they say it?' I reckon I can prise things out of people some of the time, but I could not get anything out of him on this one. He said, 'We sometimes use the word "Lord" or we sometimes use just the phrase "the Name". We say, 'You talk to the Name; the Name will hear you, and the Name will answer you.' But he said, 'No, I'm not going to use the Name.'

Jesus walked into that situation, and he said, 'When you pray, say Dad.' (That is what 'Abba' means.) In every party we take to Israel someone gets the thrill of using that word. They say, 'I just heard a child shout, "Abba, Abba".' It is the first word a Jewish child is taught. Jesus came and taught the disciples that it was not a method, technique or ritual. When you pray, say, 'Abba, Dad' —you are his child.

Now consider the use of hands when praying, because, with the exception of the mouth, that part of the body is more used in prayer in Scripture than any other part, even more than knees. Most prayer in Scripture is standing, some is kneeling, all of it is with eyes open — there is nothing in the Bible about shutting your eyes. We saw the hand being used as it should be by little beggar children at the Mount of Olives. 'Allo,' said little Arab children, and the hand was palm up, slightly cupped to catch anything that was put in, and it became almost a byword in our tour parties. How strange it is that we teach our children to do something we do not do ourselves. We teach them to use their hands in prayer. But we usually teach them the wrong posture. I have heard various explanations as to why we consider a particular way of putting hands together as being 'correct'. It is, of course, an eastern greeting to a superior. Some have said (but I do not really believe it) that you are creating a Gothic archway as a sanctuary — apparently there are some people who think they cannot pray unless the doors and windows are the shape of Gothic archways! That is not the Bible way; the Bible way is like that 'allo'; the Bible way is saying 'Dad'. Try it when you are alone. Whether you stand, kneel, sit or lie down, just try using your hands, and say, 'Dad, I need you.'

Psychologists tell us we have got to grow up and mature, get rid of father fixations and become independent. They could not be further from the truth. To mature is to change one father for another. To grow up is to change your earthly father for a heavenly one. That is what Jesus did at the age of twelve. No longer was Joseph to look after him. No longer did his little hand go into Joseph's big one. He could say: Now I am with my Father; I am in my Father's business. To grow up is not to become independent, it is to put your hand, like a child, into a bigger hand — the hand of God. That is why prayer is a simple thing. That is why God says, 'If my people will humble themselves and pray . . . .' What does he mean? If they will become like little children and put their hands up and just say this . . . . Yet a woman in my congregation said that when I raise my hands it was fascist and reminded her of the Nuremberg rallies. We are so afraid to lift hands, yet the Bible everywhere says, 'Clap your hands', and 'lift your holy hands to the Lord.' We make it into a metaphor, we spiritualise it away, but God knows we are in bodies. We are in the flesh; we are stuck with the flesh until we die. We are to pray as a whole being. So why not use your hands, keep your eyes open, and say, 'Hello, Dad.'

I will never forget a dear saint who came to Haslemere many years ago. He had a heart attack and was taken into hospital, where he died. I visited him over the last few weeks of his life. His heart was doing all sorts of silly things, and they put a pacemaker in to try to regularise it, and that did not help. He asked me to pray for him that Jesus would regularise his heart, and Jesus answered that prayer. From then on, the man had a heart that beat regularly, until he died a few weeks later. So Jesus answered one prayer, but not in the full way. In fact the man did not ask for anything more than that — just to ease that irregularity. But that man had a fragrance about him. It was not a technique, it was 'practising the presence'. One day when I went in to see him, he looked at me and said, 'Oh it's good to see you, I've just had such a lovely chat with Father.' Isn't that beautiful? Not, 'I've just said my prayers; I have just been through my quiet time.' I will never forget the way he said 'Father'. That man had tremendous faith, and it met the Fatherhood of God.

So Christian prayer begins with this sentence: 'I believe in God, the Father Almighty.' While prayer is to the heavenly Father, it is simple; it is talking, it is asking; it is coming as any little child would come to an earthly father, and saying, 'I need something and I trust you to give it to me.'

'And if you, being evil, know how to give good gifts to your children, how much more . . . .' How much more? You might like to use that as a little text or motto for your prayers this week: How much more?

PRAYER

Father, Abba, Daddy, we may be very grown up when we get on that commuter train, but we are just little children right now, and we will be then. And we need you. And, Lord, we ask in faith that you will be with us this week, that you will watch over us and look after us, that you will see us through, and that when we have any particular need, we know you will meet it because you love us. Thank you for the privilege of being able to talk to you at any time and in any place in any need — all because your Son made us his brothers, and therefore gave us permission to call you Our Father . . . in heaven, hallowed be your name. Your kingdom come. Your will be done, on earth as it is in heaven. Give us this day our daily bread. And forgive us our trespasses, as we forgive them that trespass against us. And lead us not into temptation, but deliver us from evil. For yours is the kingdom, the power and the glory, for ever and ever. *Amen*.

2

PRAYER THROUGH THE SON

Look at the following passage about the wonderful Saviour we have (Hebrews 4:12ff).

For whatever God says to us is full of living power. It is sharper than the sharpest dagger, cutting swift and deep into our innermost thoughts and desires, exposing us for what we really are. He knows about everyone, everywhere. Everything about us is bare and wide open to the all-seeing eyes of our living God. Nothing can be hidden from him to whom we must explain all that we have done. But Jesus, the Son of God, is our great high priest, who has gone to heaven itself to help us; therefore, let us never stop trusting him. This high priest of ours understands our weaknesses, since he had the same temptations we have, though he never once gave way to them and sinned. So let us come boldly to the throne of God and stay there to receive his mercy and to find grace to help us in our times of need.

The Jewish high priest is merely a man like anyone else, but he is chosen to speak for all other men in their dealings with God. He presents their gifts to God and offers to him the blood of animals that are sacrificed to cover the sins of the people and his own sins too. And because he is a man he can deal gently with other men though they are foolish and ignorant, for he too is surrounded with the same temptations and understands their problems very well. Another thing to remember is that no-one can be a high priest because he wants to be. He has to be called by God for this work in the same way that God chose Aaron. That is why Christ did not elect himself to the honour of being high priest. No, he was chosen by God. God said to him, 'My son, today I have honoured you.' And another time God said to him, 'You have been chosen to be a priest forever with the same rank as Melchizedek.' Yet while Christ was here on earth he pleaded with God, praying with tears and agony of soul to the only one who could save him from death, and God heard his prayers because of his strong desire to obey God at all times. Even though Jesus was God's Son, he had to learn from experience what it was like to obey when obeying meant suffering. It was after he had proved himself perfect in this experience that Jesus became the giver of eternal salvation to all those who obey him.

We have looked at prayer to God, focussing on two subjects: faith and Fatherhood. We now begin to think about what it means to pray *through Jesus*.

Do you remember that famous little prayer entitled *Vespers*, by A. A. Milne, in which Christopher Robin kneels by his bed and asks God to bless mummy, daddy and himself? That was what I would call a childish prayer. Nor was it in any sense a Christian prayer; it was a prayer that anybody the world over could have prayed, and Christopher Robin could have been a Buddhist, a Hindu, or whatever, and prayed that prayer. 'Christopher Robin' grew up and became the proprietor of a bookshop in Devon, and got heartily sick of people saying to him, 'Have you said your prayers today?'

Here is another prayer, which, like Christopher Robin's, came from the town of Guildford. It was written down after a Sunday evening service by a member of the congregation. It is a prayer that could only have been prayed by a Christian, and I would call it childlike rather than childish:

YOU SAID I SHOULD CALL HIM 'DADDY'

Daddy, I'm frightened and I'm scared. Daddy, it came to the end and he said about someone praying and I wanted to talk to you, Daddy. But then I got frightened and I got scared, Daddy.

There were all those people, Daddy, and I thought they'd all look at me and I'd be frightened and I couldn't say it and I'd be silly, Daddy.

I don't want to let you down or anything. I don't know all of those people, Daddy. I don't like them very much because I don't know them and they do different things, and I don't understand them, Daddy. But I wish I could have shared it with them, Daddy.

All those pictures of the children in the sunshine with their daddys. I wished I could tell them about you, and about me being a child to you. Because I can run to you and say, 'Look, Daddy, I'm running' —and I could run right into you because you are big and strong and you don't get knocked over. And I could put both my arms all round your leg, and then I can hold your hand, and you can swing me on your arm, even if you are talking to someone else. And if you are busy you can lift me right up and hold me in your arms, and I can listen to your voice if you are talking. I wish I could have told them all that, Daddy, but they are not like you, and they don't love me like you do, and they wouldn't understand. I don't love them like I love you, Daddy, because you're special, and I'm glad you're my Daddy and I didn't have to have another daddy. Because you're the best Daddy there could ever be.

The first difference between Christian prayer and all other prayer is that *we* can call God 'Daddy'. Nobody else in the world has permission to do so. Nobody else in the world is in a position to do so. Jesus, teaching disciples to pray, said,

'When you pray, say, "Daddy" . . . .' [Abba, Father].
There is a world of difference between the sort of
prayer depicted by A.A. Milne, which is childish
and just talks to God, and which anybody could
pray, whatever their religion, and the prayer
quoted above, which shows understanding of what
Christian prayer is. Prayer is universal in time and
space, but *Christian* prayer is unlike other prayer.

Some years ago I received this suggestion from
an ecumenical body: 'Why doesn't the whole
human race get together and meditate about the
divine power behind the universe? We could
link Christians and their celebration of Easter,
and Buddhists and their celebration, and other
religions. We could put them all together and we
could all meditate about the divine force behind
the universe and this would release power in the
world.' Do not believe it! Christian prayer will not
mix with other kinds of prayer. Only Christians
can come and say, 'Daddy', 'Abba', 'My Father in
heaven', and, like a little child, just say, 'Take me
into your arms, I'm here on my knees.'

The basic difference between religion and Christianity is Christ. No other religion has Christ, and

therefore 'ordinary' prayer is prayer without Christ. Christian prayer has Christ in the centre of it. I have five things to say about Christ in this context, things the Christian has in his prayer that no-one else has:

1. The Christian has the *teaching of Christ* about prayer, and there is no better teaching.

2. The Christian has the *example of Christ* in his prayer, and there is no better example to follow.

3. The Christian has the *blood of Christ* in his prayer, and there is no more powerful plea than the blood of Jesus.

4. The Christian has the *intercession of Christ*. Even as he is praying, Christ is praying for him, for he ever lives to make intercession for us.

5. Finally – and this is unique, and makes the privilege of Christian prayer so much more wonderful than the privilege of other prayer – we have the *name of Christ* to use in our prayer.

Could you ask for more? That is what makes Christian prayer so different from other prayer. And that is what makes Christian baptism so different from all other washings, because it is baptism in the name of Jesus.

First, his *teaching*. It is expected of any religious leader that he will teach his followers how to pray, and all religious leaders have done so in their different ways. Buddha did, Mohammed did, John the Baptist did. One day, the disciples came to Jesus and asked: why is it that we have been months with you and so far you have not yet taught us to pray? John taught his disciples. It is something we need help with. When are you going to start teaching us how to pray? And Jesus said: right, I'll teach you — and teach them he did. I believe he was waiting for them to ask, and that is why he is waiting for you to say, 'Lord, teach me, help me, I need help' —and the moment you ask is when he will begin to teach, but he waits for the pupil to be willing to be taught. As soon as they asked, he began to teach them.

Now the teaching he gave them about prayer is scattered teaching. He did not put it all together in a book; he did not give a long sermon on prayer; he certainly did not give a series of Sunday evening talks on prayer. What he did was to throw one hint out after another from that time onwards, as they walked.

In a party visiting Israel, a member mentioned that during the fortnight, as we walked through Galilee, they had been discipled. I was very moved by that comment and thought it was a lovely way to put it, because we found that naturally, without setting up meetings or services, we were talking about the things of God, and naturally applying a little lesson and bringing out a little object from something we had seen, in just the way that Jesus used to teach. That may be the best way to learn. I am going to string together a few bits of his teaching from many months, putting them together for you to try, and to let you see the teaching as a whole. He taught them a great deal about *how* to pray; he also taught them a great deal about *what* to pray.

HE TAUGHT THEM HOW TO PRAY

Jesus said first you must pray with **sincerity**. That is one of the most difficult things, to get sincerity into your prayer, especially in prayer meetings, and to pray as you really feel. But that is why I love that childlike prayer quoted above. That was exactly how the person felt. It was sincere, it was real; it was not going through a form of words; it was not saying things that were not true. The first thing that Jesus said on the subject is that we are to pray with sincerity, and that is why he teaches that the real test is what you say when you are by yourself. It is hypocrites who only pray in public and only say the right things in public. But he taught that the real thing is what you say to God when you are alone —how you speak to him then, when you have no prayer book and other people are not listening.

Jesus also taught disciples to pray with **simplicity**. He said, 'Don't use a lot of words.' I believe one of the biggest problems in a prayer meeting is those who can pray, not those who cannot — those who go on and on and on! I remember one dear brother in a prayer meeting who got up to pray, and he stood on the gas tap of a gas radiator in a church hall, and we began to smell it. He went on and on and on, and I wondered whether I could lift his foot up and turn the tap off, then finally he said 'Amen' —and we dashed for the door!

Jesus said, 'Do not think that because you heap a whole lot of long prayers you will be heard. That is what the Gentiles do and you must not be like them.' He then taught them a prayer that was just one minute long. He taught that simplicity is a key to prayer as well as sincerity. A simple prayer does not need to be dressed up in a whole lot of language — not long words, no parade, no paraphernalia. I remember Gordon Bailey who, when he was talking about this matter of sincerity and simplicity in prayer, said, 'Can you imagine a little boy who has got his thumb jammed in the door saying: O Dad, make haste to help me!' You just cannot imagine it. We should talk to the Lord in the way we talk to our earthly father —sincerely, simply.

We must pray with **humility**. Jesus told a story about two men who went to pray and one man had a great time of prayer — he prayed *with himself.* That is why he thought it was a great prayer, and it was just full of the personal pronoun 'I'. He stood there at the front and said, 'Lord, I thank you that I am not as other men are; I fast twice in the week; I give tithes of all that I possess.' He had a great time of prayer, with himself, says Jesus. That was as far as his prayer got. It got from his head to his heart, and he was very pleased with it. But at the back was a man who was broken, a man who beat his chest and said, 'God be merciful to me, a sinner.' Jesus said that it was the man at the back who went home having got through to God.

Pray with **tenacity**. Hold on; go on knocking —that does not mean long prayers but it does mean frequent prayers. Go on asking until you get through and get your answer.

Pray with **intensity**. Watch, and sometimes fast. It is not the length of the prayer, it is the depth of it that Jesus is concerned about.

Pray with **charity**. How can you ask God to show his love to you if you are unwilling to show his love to someone else? How can he forgive you if you are unforgiving to someone else? It just cannot be done; the circuit is incomplete; there is no link-up. It is only as your hand stretches out to your brother that you can have the flow of God's power and love into your life.

Pray with **unanimity**. When two or three agree on earth, then God will listen and he will give it to you. It is not a bad check on our prayers to ask others to pray for the same thing with us.

HE TAUGHT THEM WHAT TO PRAY

Jesus taught disciples to pray for other people. It is interesting that he singled out four groups of people for which we ought to pray and, funnily enough, we often forget to pray for them. The first we do not forget so much: he taught his disciples to pray for the sick, because prayer is a power of healing — but he also taught them to pray for those who are possessed, those who are in the grip of evil. Do you pray for such people? Thirdly, he taught disciples to pray for missionaries, labourers in the harvest field. Fourthly, he said, 'Pray for your enemies.' How often do you pray for your enemies? It is a particular category Jesus told you to pray for, and he gave a perfect example on the cross himself. 'Father, forgive them, for they know not what they do.' Stephen was the first one recorded in Scripture to take up that prayer and pray for his enemies —as they stoned him to death. Jesus also taught prayer for yourself. You have needs. You should pray for such practical things as your daily food and your clothes. You should pray for forgiveness —that is one of your daily needs. You should pray for guidance. You should pray when you are being tempted. You should pray for Holy Spirit power. All these are things you should pray for yourself. I do not know that he ever told us to pray for safety, or comfort, or even relatives — though I see no reason why we should not. I just point out the particular things that he told us to pray for. We should make sure that we include those.

Jesus also taught his disciples to pray for things for God. There are things that he wants. He wants his name to be hallowed. He wants his will to be done; he wants his kingdom to come. Pray for those things. You can make up a list from our Lord's teaching of things to pray for yourself, things to pray for others and things to pray for God, and you have got quite a list already. The first thing that we have in Christian prayer is the teaching of Jesus and I commend this to you: go through his teaching in a copy of the New Testament, and mark everything that he says about prayer in the same colour, and you will learn a whole lot.

In Christian prayer, we not only have Jesus' *teaching*, we have his *example*. He practised what he preached. I am not sure that I like the word 'example' because I do not think Jesus prayed to give us an example — I think he prayed because he needed to. But he is a glorious example. So I went through the life of Jesus to see if I could find a pattern, and I discovered there is no *pattern* in the prayer life of Jesus. He had a pattern of going every Sabbath to the synagogue, as his custom was. But it never says that he prayed at a certain hour of day as his custom was. I began to ask: when did he pray? And I discovered there were certain occasions when Jesus prayed. Below are some of them.

When he was in a big conflict or had to make a decision, he prayed. When he was going to have to choose twelve apostles, he spent all night praying about it. That does not mean he spent every night and all night in prayer, but he had a big decision to face so he prayed. I find that he prayed at all the crises and great moments of his life: at his baptism, at his transfiguration, before his death on the cross.

I notice, too, that he always prayed when he was full of emotion, whether it was emotion of great joy or great sorrow, great excitement, anger or anguish. He prayed whenever his emotions were filling him up — any kind of emotion. Now that is a very good pointer to prayer: when you are full of emotion, pray that God will help you to handle it. Do you remember the occasion when the disciples came back and said, *'Even the devils are subject to us'* —and he was so excited, so thrilled, he was filled with joy? He turned his joy into prayer in a moment and said, *'Father, I thank you that you have hidden it from the wise, and revealed it to babes and sucklings.'* He was so full of joy that he just had to pray.

So he learned to control his emotions in prayer, and to hand his feelings straight over to God in prayer. That is a pattern we might well follow, whether we are on the mountain top or in the valley bottom.

Next, I notice that he prayed particularly when he was in a crowd, or very busy. When a lot of things were pressing in on him, he used to seize a moment to pray in that situation.

Then I notice that he nearly always prayed when he was about to perform a miracle, when he was being faced with a tremendous need, when he knew that power was going to go out of him, that he would need a supply of heavenly resources. He prayed before he tackled the situation.

Am I giving you a pattern? It is not a regular 'alarm clock' pattern, it is real prayer related to real needs, real situations, real emotions — it is a way of life, and that is what I find in his life. Practising the presence rather than mastering the mechanics. Sometimes it was early in the morning, sometimes it was late at night, sometimes it was all night, but his prayer was related to life and was utterly real.

If I ask 'where did he pray?' I find that, when he could, he got away from people, and since he had no home of his own he had no bedroom of his own, so Jesus used the great outdoors, time and time again. May I suggest, if one of your problems is that the family is on top of you, or that you are in an apartment with others and you just cannot get time alone, that you go for a walk out of doors with Jesus. Do what he did and get away.

In the days of his flesh, the Bible says, Jesus offered up prayers and supplications with loud cries and tears, and he was heard for his godly fear.

Why did he pray? He prayed for other people's sake. He said, *'Lord, for their sakes, that they may believe that you are doing this, that it is for your glory. I pray for their sakes.'* He also said, *'For your sake I pray.'* But, above all, I believe that Jesus prayed for his own sake, and that if he needed to pray then it would be rash of anyone else to say 'I don't need to.' So Jesus prayed. Where? When? Why? The answers are there for you in Scripture. I commend to you his prayer in John chapter 17. It is the most marvellous prayer you have ever heard, and it is the one whole prayer of Jesus that we have. He is concerned with only two things: the glory of his Father, and the growth of his followers. What a prayer! It is full of requests and it was written down by a man who, sixty years later, vividly recalled every word of that prayer, as Jesus prayed for the glory of his Father and the growth of his followers —those are two fine things to pray for.

Not only have we got Jesus' *teaching*, not only have we got his *example*, but thirdly, when we are praying we have his *blood*, and how much we need it! Let me give you a homely illustration. There are times when I am doing something to the car.

I love messing about with my hands, and it is very therapeutic for me to do so. I get all oily and messy, and then suddenly I find that I need some bolts or some self-tapping screws. So what do I do? I knock at the kitchen door and say, 'You're not going down to the shop are you?'

'Why?'

'Well, because I can't go like this. I'll have to spend a lot of time getting this stuff off before I can go and get them. I'm just not clean enough to trot along to the shops to get what I need.' It is a simple and rather silly little illustration. Did you ever stop to think that you are just not fit to go and ask for anything from God — that you are messy; that you are dirty? How are you ever going to go into his presence and pray? *Who shall ascend the hill of the Lord — he who has clean hands and a pure heart.* How am I going to get there? There is one very simple way. Somebody has called this text the Christian's bar of soap: *The blood of Jesus cleanses from all sin.* So, when you come to pray, how about washing those hands, and that heart, in the blood of Jesus?

There is a retired army officer who before he

reads his Bible, always goes to the bathroom and washes his hands. I find that very touching, though I am not recommending you copy him. It is something that sprang out of his desire to be clean when he came to God. It is a simple thing. You have got the blood of Jesus, and that is why you can dare to come straight into his presence; even if you are dirty you can claim that blood straight away —and come clean, quite literally. For whoever confesses, God is just and he will forgive —and the blood of Jesus cleanses. So you can come clean.

There is something more. You come into a realm where there will be evil. You come into the heavenly places with your prayer. What many people do not understand is that Satan is not down there in hell, he is up there in heaven. Ephesians chapter 6 tells you this. As soon as you get into the heavenly places, you are aware of evil there, and you are in the battle —for to pray is to get into the front line of the battle. What do you do about that? Here is where the blood of Jesus comes right in again. For there is no power like the blood of Jesus against evil —no power that can keep it at bay like claiming the blood of Jesus. So you have got the blood to cleanse you, and you have got the blood to keep evil off you while you pray and battle through. That is something that no other religion can offer you, because no other religion has the blood of Jesus.

Fourthly, you have the *intercession* of Jesus. On Ascension Day we remember the most incredible thing. I have been told, and encyclopedias record, that Yuri Gagarin was the first man to go into space —rubbish! Enoch was probably the first, Elijah certainly did, and Yuri Gagarin never went into space. He had to wrap a bit of earth around himself as well as taking enough of earth's atmosphere and food even to get up there.

But I tell you that Jesus Christ, at his ascension – and I have stood on the very spot on the Mount of Olives – just stepped out into space as easily as I write this now, and he went right up to space, right up to highest heaven, and he sat down in the control room of the universe —and that is where he sits. What is he doing there, apart from controlling everything that happens, apart from having all governments under his hands, apart from having all authority and power in heaven and earth given to him? He is praying for you —and if nobody else was praying for you, he would be. Do you find that exciting? When you pray, you are joining your prayer to his; he is praying all the time; he is always interceding for you. He did it while he was on earth. He said, *'Simon, Simon, I have prayed for you that Satan would not get you.'* Do you think he stopped praying for Simon when he went back to heaven? Far from it, he just went on praying. As he always lives to make intercession, you always have somebody praying for you, so never feel that you are forgotten. If you are a Christian, then Christ is interceding for you; he does not forget one of his followers, and we can claim that.

There are two things to note here. The first is his sympathy. He prays with tremendous sympathy. Why? Because he was, and is, a man. A dear Roman Catholic lady came to one of our services. We were chatting away and I said to her, 'Why do you pray to Mary?' and she said, very simply and sincerely, 'Because she is human.' But Jesus is human, and he understands; it is when you only emphasise his divinity and forget his present humanity – and Christians often forget this – that you have to search around for someone else in heaven who is human to feel that your prayers are understood.

I do not pray to Mary —I do not need to, I pray to Jesus, he is human and he understands. He has been tempted, as I have; and he has tremendous sympathy.

A friend of mine was conducting a meeting in a Methodist church in Australia, and at the end of the meeting he invited anybody who had a need to come forward and kneel at the communion rail and ask Jesus to meet that need. A little nun in a black and white habit came up to the front, and this is what she said: 'Lord Jesus, fill me with your Holy Spirit, and if you don't I'll tell your mother of you!' That was prayer! I can tell you that Jesus was not having her pray to his mother any more, so he answered it on the spot, and he filled her to overflowing with his Spirit, right there and then.

Jesus sympathises. You do not need anybody else in heaven. You do not need saints; you do not need anyone. You have one high priest, who knows our infirmities and understands what we have been through, because he has been through it — the very worst that you could face, he has been through it. What a privilege it is to have a sympathetic and a supplicating high priest! He is on our side, as it were, but he is also on God's side. There is only one mediator between God and man – the man Christ Jesus – and in the control room of the universe there is a man right now – Jesus Christ – interceding for us.

He is able for all time to save those who draw near to God through him, since he always lives to make intercession for them (Hebrews 7:25).

Christ who died, raised from the dead, at the right hand of God, who indeed intercedes for us (Romans 8:34).

If anyone does sin we have an advocate with the Father, Jesus Christ the righteous (1 John 2:1).

It is all there, right through every writer of the New Testament. There is a song entitled *Jesus the crucified pleads for me*—a title which says it perfectly. What a lovely song that is. (To Stainer's *Crucifixion*, that beautiful tune.)

You have one more thing in Christian prayer that nobody else has. On one night in history the whole of prayer was changed. It was the night before

Jesus died, and five times that night he said one thing about prayer which has changed the whole course of prayer for millions. He had never said it before, in three years. He said—

'You can ask him for anything using my name and I will do it. For this will bring praise to the Father because of what I, the Son, will do for you. Yes, ask anything using my name and I will do it' (John 14:13f).

'but if you stay in me and obey my commands you may ask any request you like and it will be granted' (15:7).

'I appointed you to go and produce good fruit always so that no matter what you ask for from the Father, using my name, he will give it to you' (15:16).

'At that time you won't need to ask me for anything for you can go directly to the Father and ask him and he will give you what you ask for because you use my name. You haven't tried this before, but begin now, ask using my name, and you will receive and your cup of joy will overflow' (16:23).

He had taught them to pray, but he had never told them this before. The night before he died, he taught them that from now on there was something new in their prayer life. From now on they were to use his name. What did he mean? Alas, we think that all he did was give us a number of sticky labels with the name 'Jesus' on, or with the words 'through Jesus Christ our Lord', so that after every prayer we could stick it on and it is through —no more than a label on a parcel. That is not what he meant!

I think I can best explain by telling you about two very common uses of a name, which I think will help you to understand. First, imagine that I am holding out before you my cheque book. At the moment, if I filled in a cheque for you it would not bounce. That piece of paper is worthless until it has a particular name on it. I want you to imagine two more things. First I want you to imagine that my name has an overdrawn account, and that I have had a letter from my bank manager telling me that is enough —my overdraft is too big, so from now on that is it. You could use my name, I could write it, I could give you a cheque —and nothing would happen. It very much depends on the credit behind the name, does it not? As my credit is good at the moment, learning that you are in need I could in fact say, 'Right, I'll give you a cheque. I'll write my name on it, you can fill the figure in. Take it, you'll get your money and you'll be out of trouble.' A cheque is absolutely useless without a name that has credit to it.

Now I want you to apply that to the bank of heaven. Quite simply, there is not a single name that has a credit balance in the bank of heaven – not one – except the name of Jesus. No one else has any credit, everyone else has a red balance in heaven. 'Forgive us our debts.' You are in debt to God. You have overdrawn on his goodness more than he has ever received from you, so your name on a prayer will not get through, because the overdraft has been drawn. A double line has been drawn on your name. But there is someone whose credit is good: everything belongs to Jesus —everything! Everything is to his credit, to his glory; the silver and the gold is his; the cattle on a thousand hills are his, and his 'credit' is good. 'If you ask in my name' —in other words, with my signature, it will not bounce. My credit is good in the bank of heaven – that is where the treasure is

– and if you use my name you will get what you ask for. That is an amazing promise. Does it mean that Jesus has given me a book of blank cheques, all of which have been signed or stamped by his name, so that I can then simply fill in whatever I like, and feed the cheque through? No, it does not mean that, and that is why it does not work that way, and if you have tried that it would not have worked.

Many years ago, in the closing era of the old USSR, three hundred thousand names on a petition were presented to the Soviet embassy by a Member of Parliament, Michael Alison, and that petition with almost a third of a million names was refused by the embassy. It was turned away, and not one of those names could get that petition through. But imagine for one moment that at the top of the petition had been one name — Brezhnev, the Soviet leader at that time. You would not have needed all the other names. That one name would have got that petition right into the embassy! The name of Jesus is not a signature that has already been put to a book full of blank cheques, it is a signature that you must seek for your petition.

So what is it to pray in Jesus' name? It is to bring

a petition and say, 'Jesus, will you sign it?' You only need one name on your petition and it will be accepted, but it has to be a petition that he will gladly sign with his name. When that goes through to his Father, with his name on it, you do not need any more names. 'Whatever you ask in my name' —can you get Jesus to sign your petition?

There are some petitions which Jesus could not possibly sign. James and John were brothers, fishermen. They had a petition they wanted to present to God, and they came to Jesus for his signature to the petition. They said: when the kingdom of God comes, we want the two chief seats, on the right and the left. Jesus could not sign that petition and pass it on. So they could not pray it in his name, and they did not get their petition through to God. So to pray *in his name* is to stop and ask, 'Jesus, could you sign what I am asking for? Would you put your name on this petition? It's the only name that will get it through.' Jesus teaches: If you can get my signature, then you'll have it.

That is both the problem and the privilege of Christian prayer. If you can get his name on your petition, you will get it. There are many petitions he would love to sign if only you would present them. There are many prayers he would love to pass on if you would ask. There are other prayers about which he will tell you, 'I can't sign that.' There was even one occasion when he was tempted himself to offer a petition and then he realised he could not sign it himself. He said, *'Father if it be possible, take this cup from me.'* Then he realised he could not put his name to that prayer, so he rubbed it out and put another prayer: *'In spite of that, not my will but yours be done.'* He signed his name to that one, and God answered it and did his will through Jesus.

Our prayer is in the name of Jesus, and that is not a rubber stamp. The Father cannot say no to the signature of Jesus on a petition, and that is why we pray through Jesus to the Father. Somebody once said to me, 'But that makes me feel one step removed from God, if I pray through Jesus to the Father.' No, it is just the opposite. If you pray through Jesus, you will feel nearer to God than you did before you used his name. Why? Because Jesus *is* God. That is why you can pray to him, and that is why people came and prayed to him and

worshipped him, and he accepted their worship
—because he is God. So when I pray through Jesus
I am not just praying through a sympathetic man,
I am praying through the Son of God; I am praying
to the very godhead.

So Christian prayer is through Jesus, to the
Father; it uses a name; it uses blood; it uses
intercession; it uses teaching; it uses an example;
it is *Christ*–ian prayer. Christ is at the very heart
of it, so I can come and say, 'Father, you are Jesus'
Father, and through him you are mine too.' For no
man comes to the Father but by Jesus, and I am
through. I am in communication with God. Some
people say, 'I have difficulty visualising God; I have
difficulty imagining him. I know you have taught
us to call him Daddy but I just can't see the face.
How do I do that?' The answer to that is: start by
talking to Jesus. Ask him to introduce you to his
Daddy, and see what happens. Do not say 'God'
first, say 'Jesus'. And say, 'Jesus, will you take me
to your Dad, and will you put your signature to
this petition?'

3

PRAYER IN THE SPIRIT

The Bible nowhere says that prayer is easy, because it is not a natural thing. It is a natural thing to do in an emergency, but in normal, regular life when things are going smoothly it is an unnatural thing, it cuts against the flesh. An apt text would be, *We know not how to pray as we ought* .... We try, and we realise then how little we know. If you have not tried, of course, you may think you can pray, but if you have, you know you cannot. We need help. In the days of his flesh, people could go right to Jesus and get help. They could say, 'Lord, teach us to pray, we need help.' When Jesus left the earth he said: it's going to be much better for you if I go away, because someone else will come and take my place, and he will help you better than I can. He sent the Holy Spirit, and one of the things the Holy Spirit does is to help you at the point of your greatest need —which is the need to pray. *We know not how to pray as we ought*, but the next words in that verse are, *but the Spirit helps us in our weakness*. What could be more delightful?

Do you realise that God is not wanting you to struggle, he is wanting to help? The Father wants to help by listening all the time, the Son wants to help by praying for you all the time and putting a signature to your petition, and that is not where the help ends — the Holy Spirit wants to help at this end by getting the prayer going in the first place. What more help could you ask than the Holy Spirit praying in you, Jesus waiting to catch it and pass it on, and the Father waiting to receive it? A Christian has all the help he could ask for, if he makes use of it.

The prepositions we use are very important: we pray *to* the Father, *through* the Son, *in* the Spirit, *against* the devil, *with* the saints, *by* ourselves.

How do you pray in the Spirit? Here are two more texts. In Ephesians 6:18, which follows on from the armour of God passage – *Pray at all times in the Spirit, with all prayer and supplication* – it is not simply prayer, it is something else *with* all prayer and supplication. So praying *in the Spirit* is a dimension added to 'all prayer and supplication'. You may have got no further in your prayer life than all prayer and supplication, but we are now talking about this added dimension of praying *in the Spirit* with all prayer, in other words putting a new dimension to every other prayer. The brief but intriguing letter of Jude, a very relevant one for today, says: *pray in the Holy Spirit.* In fact it is more important that you should pray in the Spirit than that you should pray in the bedroom, in the church, or wherever else. The best place to pray is in the Spirit. It is an immediately accessible place wherever you are: in the office, driving your car, anywhere. That is the sphere of prayer; it does not really matter what building you are in, but the sphere does matter — praying in the Spirit.

Now I have mentioned many of the difficulties that we have in prayer. There is the difficulty of talking to someone we cannot see, hear or touch; the difficulty of knowing what to say when we feel we do get through; the difficulty that what we want to ask for may not be what we really need, and may indeed be bad for us, and there is the problem of wandering thoughts. You can make a long list of the problems, but one of the most basic ones is knowing what to say. When the disciples said, *'Lord, teach us to pray'*, they were saying: Lord teach us a prayer. Will you give us a form of words? Will you put the prayer together for us, because when we get through we really do not know what to say; we do not quite know what phrases to put together. And the Lord's Prayer was given in response to this.

What do we say? In the Middle East, even when you knew what to say to someone, if you wanted to write a letter you had to go down a street to a little man sitting at a street corner with a pen and a brass ink stand – a fascinating character, the 'letter writer'. He has some paper, he takes a pen, you dictate in one ear, and he writes it down for you. A letter writer says: you may not be able to express yourself, you tell me what you want to say and I will put it down for you and send it on for you. If I could put it this way, the Holy Spirit is the divine 'letter writer'. He takes what we want to say and cannot get out and cannot express, and he writes it down for us and he sends it on, which is delightful —to have an in-built 'letter writer' all the time.

Now prayer in the Spirit has two distinct aspects and I will try to define them for you. There is prayer in the Spirit, when he takes over your mind and gives you the right thoughts which you then have a responsibility to express. That is one kind of prayer in the Spirit — when you are praying what he has put in your mind. There is another form of prayer in the Spirit in which he does not use your mind at all but takes over your mouth, and you have the responsibility to move your mouth and your tongue. But in this case your co-operation is simply to use your mouth. So in the one case it is the Spirit acting on your mind and you taking the responsibility of translating 'mind into mouth'. In the other case your responsibility is to forget your mind and let him have your mouth and use it. The second kind of prayer is very difficult for some people but, once they have learned it, it is a very beautiful kind of prayer. Both these kinds of prayer are praying in the Spirit. Without praying in the Spirit, prayer is simply telling God what you feel you want, or what you feel is needed in the situation — it is coming from your mind *and* your mouth. You can then offer it through Jesus to the Father. But, in both cases, praying in the Spirit is where he is giving you the right thoughts to express or has bypassed your mind and is giving you the actual words. He does not pray *for* you — it says he *helps* us in our weakness, it does not say he takes over and does it for us.

There is one big problem that many people have about praying in the Spirit. One dear lady said to me, 'I have been praying for the gift of praying in another language.' I replied, 'What have you been doing?' She said, 'Well, I have been kneeling by my bed, I have been asking and asking, and then I have opened my mouth. I have just waited for something to come and nothing has ever come.' That is not surprising. If you have prayed in this way, you will understand perfectly well why nothing ever came. The Holy Spirit does not pray *for* us, he *helps* us, and in fact he prays *with* us, and we need to co-operate with him if we are going to pray in the Spirit. The Greek prepositions used in Romans chapter eight, where it says that we know not how to pray as we ought, but the Spirit helps us with our infirmity, tell us that he does not help us *out of* it, he helps us *in* it and with it, and enables us to overcome it. That is the delightful part that he plays.

Now let us take the influence of the Spirit on the mind — what I would call *mental prayer*, the prayer of the mind in which your mind is fully involved with conscious thoughts, which the Holy Spirit has placed there in some way, whether through an impression, a burden or a memory, or through a circumstance, but the Lord himself, the Holy Spirit, has put within your mind that for which you ought to pray. When you do not know what to pray for, why not ask him to tell you what to pray for? When you know someone is in need and you do not know that need, why not ask him to tell you what the need is? You will be astonished how often he can put the thought into your mind that is absolutely right on the button for that person — and it may not be their most obvious need.

When we are praying in the Spirit in this mental way, the brain is involved and the mind is active.

The Spirit helps us not only with the mind but with the heart and the will, so your whole personality is quickened. Here there are three problems. The first is that with my heart I do not have a strong enough desire to pray. Quite simply, we tend to do everything that we really want to do. If you really want to do something, you will usually find a way to do it. So my first problem is with my heart: that I obviously do not want enough. Secondly, there is a problem with my mind: wandering thoughts; difficulty with concentrating — trying not to think about yesterday's football match! My third problem is my will — sheer discipline. I can desperately try to work up a desire and feelings; I can desperately try to keep my thoughts in the right direction; I can desperately try to discipline my will. But this desire, direction and determination are not easily come by, and you need a pretty strong personality to achieve them.

It is precisely at this point that the Holy Spirit says: let me help you with these three areas; let me give you passion in your prayer; let me give you perception in your prayer; let me give you persistence in your prayer. Have you ever thought of asking for those three things? 'Lord, give me a passion to pray so that my heart wants to; give me perception, so that my mind knows what to ask for; and give me persistence that will keep on asking until I get it.' The Holy Spirit wants to deal with your whole personality, and help you at each of those points.

You can always tell when someone is praying in the Spirit, even when their mind is involved and is thinking hard, because three things will come through. First, the will of the Father will come through — because the Holy Spirit helps us in our weakness and he prays with us according to the will of the Father. We note here something vital: do not add 'if it be your will' as a kind of codicil, a cover-up clause at the end of your prayer. Rather, we are to know the will of God and to pray the will of God. If you are praying in the Spirit you know the will of God. The Holy Spirit prays in the will of the Father, and when the Spirit is helping your thoughts in prayer you will have the will of the Father clear in your mind — you will prove his will. It is good and acceptable and perfect.

Secondly, if the Spirit is in your mental prayer

then the glory of Jesus will be in it too. *'He came to glorify me'*, says Jesus, and you will find that if someone is praying in the Spirit their thoughts will uplift the Lord Jesus. That is another change he makes to the thoughts of someone praying in the Spirit.

The third thing he will do is this: when someone is praying in the Spirit, into their prayer will come not quotable quotes but echoes of God's Word, because the Spirit wrote the Bible. He never contradicts himself and he will pull the sword of the Spirit out of the belt of truth, again and again, in someone who is praying in the Spirit.

Now do you see the difference between an unbeliever praying, however sincerely, and someone praying in the Spirit? An unbeliever will pray for the things they feel are needed. They will pray for what they want, they will address God, they may even say 'through Jesus Christ our Lord', and 'if it be thy will', but the thoughts of someone praying in the Spirit will be clear about the will of the Father and the glory of the Son and the truth of Scripture. The Spirit will bring those three notes in prayer.

So this is the help the Spirit wants to give you at the mental level: directing your mind in prayer; giving a desire in your heart to pray; giving a perception in your mind, so that you know what is the will of God; giving a determination of the will to go on asking until you receive it; leading you to exalt Jesus and draw from the truth of Scripture and seek the will of God. It all seems to fit together in the pattern. It means that I am responsive and open to him in my mind, and listening mentally to get what the Spirit is saying to me —so that the prayer becomes not *my* mental prayer but *his* mental prayer and I am thinking the Spirit's thoughts after him before I express them. Now that is one form of praying in the Spirit. You will recognise it in a prayer meeting, you will recognise it in a church.

The other kind of praying in the Spirit is becoming known to many more Christians today. In this kind of prayer, as Paul says, the mind is 'unfruitful', or literally, 'unproductive'. In other words, in this kind of prayer in the Spirit there are no thoughts at all. The Holy Spirit takes over at another level — he takes over at the mouth level, and he prays a prayer that is beautiful, which you have not had to think up. It is a sheer relief sometimes to be able to pray a prayer that you have not had to think up, or that you have not had to wrestle through with the Spirit to get in terms of thought from him — especially when you are tired and when you find it difficult to pull your thoughts together.

It is a form of prayer that comes in very useful when you are busy doing other things and need your mental concentration elsewhere. For example, the kind of prayer I have been writing about thus far would be very dangerous to exercise while you are driving because your mind would be concentrating on the traffic — it ought to be, anyway! If you are praying mental prayer while you drive and you are trying to get his thoughts into your mind while you drive, you are a dangerous driver — as dangerous as if you were filled with another kind of spirit! But you can pray the prayer in the Spirit that is mouth only and lose no mental concentration whatsoever, and pray while you drive perfectly safely, or while you do the washing up, or while you are doing another job, or when you just do not know what to pray or are stuck for words completely. I think it is most lovely and gracious of God ever to think of giving us such a help in prayer. It is beautiful.

What does a prayer that has not come from someone's mind sound like? Some prayer in the Spirit may sound to you like a groan. Recall Romans chapter eight: *we know not how to pray as we ought, but the Spirit helps us in our weakness.* How? What form of prayer? What comes out? *With words that cannot be uttered.* Now the Greek word translated 'uttered' here does not mean noise, it does not mean 'sounded'. It means *to put something into words.* On the day of Pentecost they were all filled with the Holy Spirit and they began to speak as the Holy Spirit gave them utterance. The word means 'form of words'. It does not mean that the Holy Spirit made their voice box go – that is their responsibility – it means the Holy Spirit shaped their tongues and mouths to turn the sounds into words. And indeed that is one of the secrets of this kind of prayer, that you make the noise and the Holy Spirit shapes it. But Paul writes of *groans that cannot be uttered*, and sometimes the Holy Spirit enables you to pray with a groan that cannot be put into words at all, neither your own language nor any other — but just a sheer groan, and it is a prayer, and a strong prayer. I wonder if you have ever prayed that kind of prayer and just groaned. Look through the Bible to see how often the Lord hears the people groaning.

If you have ever been in an earthquake, you will have heard the earth, the rocks, groaning. Towards the end of history there are going to be more and more earthquakes, and Romans 8, the same chapter in the same context of our groans that cannot be put into words, says the whole creation is groaning. There are groans coming up from nature itself, which is waiting for God to redeem the whole of nature including our bodies — a new heaven and a new earth. We are thinking big! Have you got that big in your thinking yet?

Sometimes your longings, burdens and passions are so deep and you cannot put them into words. Even the Spirit cannot put them into words for you, so if he enables you to groan, that is a kind of prayer.

Another form of prayer in the Scripture that is from the mouth and does not come from the mind is a sigh. Have you ever noticed a sigh in

Scripture, and how God listens to sighing? Have you ever sighed? That can be prayer. Our view of prayer can be too narrow when we limit it to verbal communication.

Tears can be another form of prayer. When you cannot get it into words and the Holy Spirit does not put it into words, sometimes you can do nothing but weep. Have you prayed in that way before? No words, just tears. In the Middle East when someone is bereaved, relatives who have wept for them in their sorrow have little glass bottles and they catch the tears, and instead of sending a wreath to the funeral they send a bottle of tears. I think that is more meaningful than a wreath. The psalmist says, *Put my tears in your bottle, O Lord.* That is prayer! And God has a bottle to catch a tear. The Holy Spirit can lead us to many forms of prayer which are not even uttered, which are never put into words — a groan, a tear, a sigh are not put into words.

Then there are other kinds of prayer in which your mind is not involved but in which ejaculations do occur in a word or a phrase. Let us think of some of them. *Abba* is one. Have you ever found yourself shouting that? Not 'Daddy' — that is the English translation. Have you ever heard yourself actually saying 'Abba'? It says that the Spirit is bearing witness with your spirit, that you are a son of God. Why? Because it is the Spirit of the Son of God in you using your mouth to address his own Father in his favourite way in the Aramaic language — 'Abba'. And that is why it is kept in the original Aramaic in every English translation. It is not when you cry 'Daddy', it is when you cry 'Abba', which is Jesus calling to his own Father through your mouth. And my, you really know you are a child of God when you cry 'Abba'. When you shout out 'Abba', the verb is 'to cry out', and it is the verb used when the disciples saw Jesus walking on the water and they were scared stiff and they shouted out — the Greek verb is *krazein*. They *krazein*–ed! Galatians chapter 4 tells us that when you *krazein* '*Abba*', the Spirit of his Son within you is calling to his own Dad through your mouth in his original language.

Here is another ejaculatory word: *Maranatha*, which means 'come, come Lord Jesus, come back, come quickly'. Have you ever said that in your prayers without thinking about it? The Spirit of God was doing it if you did.

Now let us come to the heart of it. The Holy Spirit can not only make you groan and express your deepest longings that way, or in a sigh, or in tears, or in an ejaculation that may well be in the original language of Jesus, he can also give you total fluency in any language he knows. If there is one word I hate, and I wish I could expunge from every translation of the Bible, it is the word 'tongues'. It conveys to me a kind of babbling which is so far from the truth that I am not surprised it puts people off. Why will the translators not use the proper word? I will tell you why — because they have no idea what the experience is, and they are just guessing. So they do not translate it as they ought, and the translation in English of the Greek word is 'language', and what is wrong with 'language'? Nothing at all. So wherever you see the word 'tongues', cross it out and put in the word 'languages', and you are home and dry.

On the day of Pentecost they were all of one accord in one place and they were all filled with Holy Spirit, and they all began to speak in other languages as the Holy Spirit put the words together.

The devil hates this because he knows it sets people free in prayer, and he hates it because he knows that every word of that prayer will be just right, and that is why he will do anything he can to turn people off this, and to make other people fanatical in it so others will be put off, to get you away from it and say you do not need it, and anyway it is only for some so don't you bother about it, and don't you want it. I stand firmly with the apostle Paul — *I would that you all spoke in tongues*, especially those of you who have greater mental powers than others. I wish you could understand the simplicity of giving him your mouth and letting him pray through you and being released.

It is a prayer in which the Lord supplies every word for you. When your children were small and it was your birthday, did you give them some money to go and get a present for you? Most parents do. God said, here is a prayer to pray to me. It is only those who are prepared to become as little children and even learn what may seem like 'baby talk' who will receive such a gift, but it is a beautiful gift. If anybody decries that gift, I remind them it was the very first one that the Lord gave to his church. If you say it is the lowest, then I say that is the best one to begin with. It was a lovely gift. They had been meeting daily in a prayer meeting. That was a church of prayer, believe me: 120 people met every day for prayer. They had met every day for ten days in prayer, and they had mental prayer, but on the day of Pentecost they switched from mental prayer to a completely different kind of prayer, in which God had their mouths but not their minds, and he poured out his Spirit — and they were free and they were praising him.

This is a gift primarily for personal prayer. I would be delighted if you would all speak in tongues, but I stand firmly with the apostle Paul also in this: by conviction, I would rather speak five words in church that the congregation understand than ten thousand in another language, and that is where I stand firmly on the Scripture. That is where I believe the primary use of the gift is to help me to be released when I am stuck.

There are abuses, and there can be counterfeit. I came across one in New Zealand where somebody in public showed a gift they thought they had, and it proved to be of Satan. It was in the Maori language, which we discovered as there were Maoris present who recognised it as blasphemous and obscene. There is counterfeit, but the devil only counterfeits where the real thing is around. He does not bother to counterfeit what nobody has. There are strict scriptural limitations on this gift in public, because if I pray in another language during preaching it is going to help nobody but me. It will build me up, it will release me, but it will not help others one little bit, unless somebody translates it for them, and that is such a roundabout way of praying that it is best to limit it to two (or three at the very most) in one meeting. But I want to help you in your secret prayer as well as your public prayer, and this is a supreme gift.

I have read many books on the life of St Paul. I have even read books which contained a chapter on his prayer life — and he had a tremendous prayer life. Writers have put together from his epistles the thoughts he had on prayer and things he prayed: that his readers might be filled with the fullness of God; that they may prove the length and breadth and height of love. Yet I have found that this particular form of prayer in Paul's experience is neglected. The astonishing thing is that he says in one of his letters to the Corinthian church – which was pentecostal, with all the trimmings and with all the abuses – *I thank God that I speak in languages more than all of you.* And there you hit the secret of Paul's power. How could he have kept going — a man who was stoned, shipwrecked, beaten, given thirty-nine stripes on more than one occasion. How did he manage? How did he support himself? Paul says that he thanks God he has this way of praying, and that he uses it more than all the Corinthians put together. Here you have touched one of the deep secrets of his life. When Paul was beaten and tired, he knew that he could pray without mental effort, and that God could just take over. Ask yourself, would I like such a gift? I praise God if you have found release in this way.

There have been some astonishing examples of incidents where languages unknown to the person, spoken by the person, have been recognized by foreign native speakers.

Here is a true story which I have recounted in membership training classes. Many years ago I was minister in a church where there was a deacon who had a great brain and had built up a big business, but he did not like me, and we did not get along. Every May or June he became ill. He had a hay fever condition coupled with an asthmatic chest, and at that time of year he would be flat on his back for six weeks. One year, when he was suffering in this way, he asked for me to go and visit him. I went on a Sunday afternoon and all the way there I kept thinking of words from James chapter five, *Is any among you sick? Let him send for the elders, let them anoint him with oil . . . let them pray.*

I had not done it before, and I thought: well, could I do it for him? When I got to his house and talked to him he looked me straight in the eyes and said, 'What do you think of James 5?'

I said, 'Well, I have been thinking about it. What do you think about it?'

He said, 'Would you do it? I have to be in Switzerland on Thursday, it's urgent for my business; I have got my air ticket. The doctors put me in bed, flat on my back, for two weeks. I have just got to go, would you consider doing it?'

I said, 'I'll consider it, I'll think it over.'

'You think it over.'

His wife rang on Wednesday morning and said, 'He wants you to come and do it.'

So I said, 'Well, I feel I ought to.'

So I rang up a few of the other deacons and asked, 'Would you mind fasting and praying today and coming with me tonight?'

I bought a little bottle of olive oil and felt a bit of a fool doing so. Then I went alone into the church, went into the pulpit where I usually stood, and I knelt to pray. I could not pray for that man. I did not want to help him. It was my mental prayer, and my thoughts about him were wrong. Then, I do not know how it happened, though I had no emotions, feelings or hysteria whatever, I suddenly began praying for the deacon as I have never prayed for anyone else in my life. I prayed and prayed, and it was all absolutely real. I knew I was praying exactly what God wanted from me. But I found that I was praying in what I assume now, from what I have heard since, was Chinese, which is certainly a language I have never learned, nor ever will — but God knows every language in the world, and the languages of the angels as well (there are languages of men and of angels), and I do not know how many languages that is! Of course, without love these languages are of no use at all, and in public use they need to be translated.

I looked at my watch and thought that it must have been an hour fast, but an hour had passed without my noticing. I still had no 'feeling', but I was praying. So I thought: well, I have another half hour, I'm going to go on praying. Sure enough, the language flowed back, and I was able to pray for the man. It was beautifully restful because my mind was at peace and at rest.

So we went to see him that night and we laid hands on him, we poured oil over his head. He lay there grey and ill, we confessed our sins, and it was pretty good to get that out. Do you know what happened when we had finished? Absolutely nothing. He lay there, and he could not even sit up. Here was my first big test. I got up, and I remember looking at him and saying, 'Well Jimmy, we have done everything we could; we have done everything the Bible says. Have you still got your air ticket for tomorrow?'

'Yes,' he replied.

'Right,' I said, 'I'll run you to the airport.' I went home and could not sleep a wink. In the morning I did not have the guts to ring him up. I tried to get on with preparing a sermon and found that I could not concentrate.

The telephone rang, and a voice said, 'Will you run me to the airport?'

I said, 'Are you all right, Jimmy?'

'I'm fine.'

'Have you been to the doctor?' I asked.

'Yes, the doctor said I can go,' he replied. 'I have even been and had my hair cut, and the barber said, "Excuse me, sir, but I think I ought to tell you your hair is getting rather greasy, so would you like a shampoo as well?"' So he was able to tell him the story of what had happened.

Now I can tell you two very simple and beautiful things. One, he has never again been troubled with that hay fever and asthma. Number two, and to me far more wonderful, we were now the closest friends — and when the Lord told me that I had to come to Guildford, and I was really being torn, and feeling my roots being pulled up, the first man I made for, to share it with, was that deacon.

That is how I discovered that there is a kind of prayer in the Spirit that God wants to help us with. If somebody says, 'Must I pray this way?' they have got the question wrong. It should be 'May I?' rather than 'Must I?' The Holy Spirit does not force you to do this if you do not want to. I love it when somebody says, 'May I?' Sadly, some people would run a thousand miles from something that is unknown, or seems to them to be peculiar, or which they just do not understand —but gifts sent from heaven are good and perfect, and this is something sent down from heaven. So do not let the devil tell you it is anything else. It is satanic work to try and stop you praying as God wants you to pray, and the enemy will tell you all kinds of strange tales to divert you from this one.

There is the practical question: how? I can tell you in two words, and I am now referring to both forms of praying in the Spirit — the form that involves your mind and the form that does not. If you want my scriptural authority for this distinction, it is in 1 Corinthians 14. Paul says, *I pray with my mind and I pray with my spirit, I sing with my mind and I sing with the Spirit.* These are two different kinds of prayer, and Paul tells us that he does both. Beware of those who only pray in tongues and never pray with the mind; beware of those who only pray in the mind and never pray with the spirit.

So how? These are the two words: 'ask' and 'receive'. Everybody who is helped in prayer has first asked. Here is a text from Luke chapter 11, which cannot apply to unbelievers because unbelievers cannot even know the Holy Spirit. It can only therefore apply to believers, and it tells them to ask for Holy Spirit. The theologians come along and say: but you are a Christian, you already have the Holy Spirit. Yes, you have the Holy Spirit the person, but you can always ask for more of him. This verse says: *'If you who are evil know how to give good gifts to your children, how much more will your heavenly Father give Holy Spirit to those who go on asking him?'*

Do you want this? Then ask until you get it, like that friend at midnight go on hammering at the door until you get it. God loves to answer bold importunity.

But there is another side, and this is where the problem so often occurs. In a sense there is a surrender involved, an act of surrender, of letting go and letting God. The one thing most of us hate to do is to let go of our self-control, because we fear that if we do we may finish in chaos or even madness. I tell you, the fruit of the Spirit is self-control, and if you get his self-control, believe me, it is much better than yours — and a genuine gift of the Spirit has no loss of self-control about it whatsoever. If it has, it is not of the Spirit. The spirit of the prophet is subject to the prophet, Paul teaches. Therefore, the Holy Spirit graciously puts this gift under your control. So no-one need ever be afraid of being rushed beyond what they control. You decide whether you let him take over or not, and if you do not like it when he takes over, you can stop it — but you will not want to.

We come now to thinking about how we receive. If I had a bar of chocolate and I held it out, you would know how to receive that, wouldn't you? I would say: here it is, ask for it and receive it. You would

know that you would have to come and take it. I
was once talking to children in a church, and I was
trying to describe grace. I had a bar of chocolate
and said, 'Here it is, for the first child who comes
and gets it.' Nobody moved. They all watched,
until one very cheeky little lad ran out, grabbed
it, and then ran back. Now he actually received
what was being offered. The biggest problem with
many people is that they ask and never receive.
Receiving involves an active grasping of something.
It involves getting over the psychological hurdle,
for example, of hearing your own voice make
sounds that you do not understand. That is a real
hurdle. You have simply got to do it until you get
over it. Some people gloriously do not have that
barrier, and they just open their mouth and start,
but others have to go on talking until the Lord
has got them over that hurdle. Then he gives
them a language, and he gives them fluency. They
may feel it is baby talk at first, because they have
never heard such things from their own mouth,
but as they go on they realise it is a language with
grammar, with syntax, and it is a language of heaven
that God is giving them to address to himself.

It is rather like Peter in the boat, when he said to Jesus, 'Could I walk on the water?' And Jesus did not say get your Bible out, claim the promises, get on your knees in the boat; pray, pray, pray, pray. No, Jesus said come on, do it! He was always doing that. To a man lying on a stretcher, he said, 'Get up, and carry that thing.' He did not say get out your Bible, read this promise, pray, pray, pray —he said do it. That is how spiritual gifts come, and you do not know if you have a gift of healing until you go and lay hands on someone.

When your spirit receives a strong impression that you could do something, why not just step out of the boat and do it? That is how such gifts come, that is how you receive. The Bible does not say that a gift of the Spirit is like brilliant piano playing, but supposing it did. How would you know if you had received it? There is only one way I know, and that would be for you to go to a piano, sit down and put your fingers on the keys —and start. You would soon know if you had received that gift or not.

May I tell you about Muriel Shepherd, who was conductor of the London Emmanuel Choir after her late husband had conducted it. One night, both

Edwin and Muriel asked the Lord to drench and fill them with his Spirit. Up to that point, Muriel could not play one note on the piano without sheet music. Some musicians can play with or without, but most are either 'ear' or 'eye' — and she was 'eye'. Disasters had occurred when she mislaid a piece of music or left it at home and she arrived at a concert — somebody else had to step in. After she was drenched in the Spirit, she said, 'Lord, would you give me a gift of playing the piano by ear?' And in the middle of the night the Lord said, 'I have given you the gift.' And right then she went downstairs and sat at the piano. She put no music in front of herself, and she played! She has played without music from that point onwards. Now how did she know she had the gift? From some promise of the Bible? From some message from heaven? No. She knew it when she went downstairs to the lounge and put her fingers on the keys. That is how you discover every other gift, and this is how you pray in the Spirit: you ask, 'Lord, I'm weak, I need your help. I need your Holy Spirit, I cannot pray as I ought.' Then receive and say, 'Lord, I believe that as I pray [if this is a mental prayer] that you

121

will put the right thoughts in my mind which will glorify you.' Jesus will be glorified, and the Spirit will draw on the truth of Scripture. But I beg you, do not stop there. There is this other kind of prayer, and you can ask, 'Lord, I am tired tonight, my mind can't put the thing together; Lord, here's my mouth and I'm just going to start talking, and you give the utterance and it will still be prayer.' Or, 'Lord, Holy Spirit, help me to cry or to sigh, or to groan, but Holy Spirit, help me to pray.'

4

PRAYER AGAINST THE DEVIL

This was written by Paul, who was imprisoned for his faith:

Last of all, I want to remind you that your strength must come from the Lord's mighty power within you. Put on all of God's armour so that you will be able to stand safe against the strategies and tricks of Satan. For we are not fighting against people made of flesh and blood, but against persons without bodies, the evil rulers of the unseen world, those mighty satanic beings and great evil princes of darkness who rule this world, and against huge numbers of wicked spirits in the spirit world. So use every piece of God's armour to resist the enemy whenever he attacks, and when it is all over, you will still be standing up. But to do this you will need the strong belt of truth and the breastplate of God's approval; wear shoes that are able to speed you on as you preach the good news of peace with God. In every battle you will need faith as your shield to stop the fiery arrows aimed at you by Satan, and you will need the helmet of salvation and the sword of the Spirit, which is the word of God. Pray all the time. Ask God for anything in line with the Holy Spirit's wishes. Plead with him, reminding him of your needs, and keep praying earnestly for all Christians everywhere. Pray for me too, and ask God to give me the right words as I boldly tell others about the Lord, and as I explain to them that his salvation is for the Gentiles too. I am in chains now for preaching this message from God, but pray that I will keep on speaking out boldly for him, even here in prison, as I should.

(Ephesians 6:10–20).

I think that one of the most extraordinary – even shocking – discoveries a Christian makes is that sometimes it is harder to pray since you became a Christian than it was as an unbeliever. You may well have had this experience. I was talking to a lady who does not go near a church and does not read her Bible, but she faithfully says her prayers every night. She would be among those who say, 'I'm just as good a Christian as those who go to church.' But the intriguing thing to me was she never had any problems in praying. She never had any barriers to get through, she just said her prayers daily. And I thought: if you became a Christian you would have problems with your prayer. I wonder why that should be. Recall what we have been thinking about so far: we have a heavenly Father to pray to; we can have faith in that Father; we have the name of Jesus, the example of Jesus, the teaching of Jesus, the blood of Jesus – so much to help us – and prayer should be so much more to the Christian than it is to anyone else — yet it really can be a greater battle than ever. But, as we noted earlier, Christian prayer is never private. It involves the Father to help, the Son to take the prayer through to intercede for us, and the Spirit —who knows that we do not know how to pray and what to say, and who is able to help us with our thoughts and our words. Yet it is a battle, because as soon as you pray you are involved with the devil, and Satan hates you for it. He doesn't mind prayers, but he hates Christian prayer, because that is what is going to do the damage to him. He is against it. He is not the slightest bit afraid of an unbeliever's prayer.

There was an American estate owner who had a slave who was a believer, and he would keep talking to his master about both the Lord and the devil. And the master said, 'Oh, the devil never bothers me.' Then, one day, the master went out shooting duck. He shot at a couple of ducks flying over and they both fell, but one clearly got most of the shot and it landed on the ground, dead. The other still had life in it and was fluttering its wings and trying to take off and go. The slave ran after the dead one to pick it up, and the master yelled after him, 'Don't go after the dead one, go after the one that's got some life in it, that's trying to fly.'

The slave turned round and said, 'Now I've just understood why you're never troubled by the devil, master. I've seen it. You see, the devil is only afraid of Christians who are trying to fly in prayer, who have got a bit of life in them. He is not worried about religion, he is not worried about prayers, but Christians who are really trying to pray in the name of Jesus, that gets him really worried. And therefore he attacks at that point.'

I have a theory that the devil is quite short! Why? Because you can sock him on the jaw best when you are on your knees! Seriously, though, while there may be a bit of humour in this book, do not underestimate the devil, and do not treat him as a joke. But as the saying goes, 'Satan trembles when he sees the weakest saint upon his knees.'

I went into a little old church in the county of Buckinghamshire once, where they were re-decorating. They had washed off the old layers of whitewash and discovered a fresco, a painting, behind it. I was intrigued by it because it was a painting of the church itself, full of people wearing medieval costume in the pews. I noticed that sitting alongside every member in this fresco, next to each Christian worshipping, was a little demon holding the member's mouth shut. That was a strange little drawing, but it spoke to me. The demons were holding the members' mouths shut so that they would remain among the silent saints who suffer from 'lockjaw'! You may know the problem, it is one found in many churches. That fresco stayed with me for a long time. I believe that when you come to know the Lord you come to know the devil at the same time. If someone says to me, 'Well, I don't have any experience of the devil; I've never come across the devil', I honestly wonder how far they have gone with the Lord. Because the devil is not in hell, he is in heaven. The book of Job makes that quite clear. He patrols the earth, but his home is heaven. So we wrestle against the powers of evil not in the hellish places but in the heavenly places —that is where they are. That is why prayer becomes a real difficulty.

The first thing in any battle is to define your enemy. You have to identify him before you decide how you can overcome him. I know of a man who in World War 1 was shot dead by British bullets, and he was a British soldier. A platoon advanced through a wood, but the lines of communication got messed up and the news of this advance was not sent back to the rest. British soldiers saw these soldiers moving through the wood and opened fire, and he was killed. You have to be sure you have identified the right enemy. Never pray against people, because you are not wrestling against flesh and blood, so human beings are not the enemies — we are wrestling against beings without bodies. We are wrestling against the devil himself in prayer, and it is a real battle.

Now let me tell you a bit about the devil, so that you have got a clear picture in your mind of what you are praying against. Christians are called not only to pray for people but to pray against certain powers, the chief of whom is Satan himself.

A Scotland Yard inspector was once asked whether he believed in a personal devil. He said straight away, 'Of course I do.'

The questioner said, 'On what grounds do you believe in the personal devil?'

'Well,' he replied, 'I am a Christian, I believe the Bible, and the Bible says there is a personal devil, so that would settle it for me, but I have had some very good evidence of the existence of a personal devil.'

'What is it?' the questioner asked.

The detective inspector continued, 'Sometimes in London there is a new outbreak of crime, and we find the little men, the boys, incapable of having planned the crime that they have committed. We know, when there is a spate of this, that there is a new king of the underworld, a new Mr X. So we open a file on Mr X. We don't know his name, we don't know where he lives, we don't know who he is. But from the crimes that he leads these petty criminals to do we build up a picture of the kind of person he must be, and gradually we gain a complete picture of his character, the kind of man we are looking for, and we know he exists although we have never clapped eyes on him. As I talk to Christians and find out how the devil gets at them and what he makes them do, I can open a file on him and I can build up a picture of his character and his strategy and his tricks and the kind of way he thinks.' He had plenty of evidence of the existence of the devil.

Let me then tell you something of what the Bible tells us about him. The Bible does not paint him as a horned creature with a forked tail — that is the kind of thing that makes us laugh at him and take him less than seriously. Have you seen Pasolini's *Life of Christ*? Incredibly, it was made by an Italian communist film director. The scene where our Lord was tempted by Satan is still vivid in my mind. Our Lord was out there in the wilderness, dressed in traditional Eastern garb. I thought: now how is Pasolini going to portray the devil? Is he going to fall for the usual caricature? Then the film looked into the distance and across the desert there was a tiny figure striding slowly, steadily, straight for Jesus. As he came nearer and you saw him, he was a highly intelligent looking, polished, smooth, well-dressed businessman. That was a brilliant touch. Here was a man you felt had power at his fingertips, a man who you felt had all the riches of the world, and who just had to say, 'Do that', and somebody would jump to it. He just strode in there and went up to Christ, and a shiver went down my spine. I thought, Pasolini has understood. He has not underestimated or caricatured or joked about Satan. You see, the Bible says that he is a real person; the Bible never calls the devil 'it', always 'he'.

Next, the Bible says that he has a heart and a mind and a will, and if a heart, a mind and a will do not make a personality, what does? It talks about the devil's feelings, thoughts and motives. That, to me, means he is a person. So the devil is not just a kind of vague word to sum up all the forces of evil in the world. I do not think that Satan is simply a name for the baser instincts of human nature. Satan is a person in his own right. If there were no human beings at all, Satan would still exist. He is a person with a heart that feels, a mind that thinks and a will that acts. God holds him morally responsible for what he does, and you cannot hold less than a person morally responsible. He has various names in Scripture: Lucifer, Beelzebub, Belial, Satan, Abaddon. They are horrible names, as you realise when you know their Hebrew meaning.

More than that, the Bible gives him descriptions. A 'snake' is one. Now some people like snakes, though I have never been able to understand why. But he is a wily serpent. He is also described in terms of a prowling lion and as a dragon. Would you like to be left in a room with a snake, a lion or a dragon? As soon as you pray in the name of Jesus, you are in a room with those three, and they are not to be thought of lightly. For that is exactly what he is. His character is also described: he is a liar, a murderer, a slanderer, an accuser, an adversary, a destroyer. Are you beginning to get the feel of him? Why is he like this? Where did he come from? Did God create him? Yes, God created him, but just as God created man good and then man decided not to be, so God created Satan good and he has known what 'good' is. For the Bible talks very clearly and says that Satan was and is an angel, which is a higher order of created being than man. I found it intriguing when Billy Graham wrote a book on angels. Twenty years before that, people would not have bought a book on angels, but something changed. Now we are aware there is a supernatural world.

So Satan was an angel, and he was in heaven with God, and he used to be good. Why then did he decide to go the way he did? He decided to go that way for the same reason that we decide to go that way: he wanted something for himself rather than for God. And he wanted to be able to say, 'Mine is the kingdom and the power and the glory, for ever and ever.' He wanted to change one word in the Lord's Prayer — 'mine' instead of 'thine'. If you trace back human rebellion against God, you can trace it back to the same motive: to be able to say 'mine' instead of 'thine'.

Now his motive therefore is primarily pride, which is sin, and which in turn leads to hatred, and hatred leads you to be destructive, and to want to break down rather than to build up. Therefore Satan now has an exclusively destructive role in society.

Jesus himself took Satan desperately seriously. He never made a joke about him; he never laughed at him; he never caricatured him. Consider some of the titles Jesus gave Satan. He said he is the prince of this world. When Satan offered Jesus all the kingdoms of the world, Jesus did not say they are not yours to give, because he knew perfectly well they were Satan's to give. It is a horrible thought, if you really realise it, that the world in which we live is ruled over by Satan. He is the prince of this world, but let us take it a step further. Do you know another title that Jesus gave to Satan? He not only spoke of him as ruler or prince of this world, but as the 'god' of this world. The only other person besides his heavenly Father to whom Jesus ever applied that word was Satan. He taught that his own heavenly Father is God of everything, but of this world Satan is god, which means, very simply, not only that Satan controls this world and is able to manipulate science and education and politics for his own ends; more than that, Satan is actually the real god who most people on earth worship, whether they know it or not. Behind so much religion, behind so much activity, Satan is the one who is being worshipped — even by some who go to church and chapel on Sunday. In reality he is their god, for they worship the things that he offers them. They want the things of the world that he belongs to and rules over, rather than setting their minds on the things that are above, where Jesus is. And if you want *this* world and if you want the things of this world, then I give you a piece of advice: make Satan your god. If you want this world then he is a wonderful god to have, because he will give them to you, but there is only one snag — there is always a price to pay, and when the bill comes in you may not be quite so happy. But he will give it to you. He can give you money, fame, anything you want, because it is his to give. *'Where have you been, Satan?'* says God in the book of Job. *'I have been patrolling the earth.'* He had been looking around his estate.

Now let us be clear, that does not mean that God is helpless in this world. It does mean – and we must think this through – that God is allowing Satan to be prince of this world and god of this world. He has allowed it. People ask: what does God think he is doing, allowing that? My answer to that is: what is he doing, allowing *you* to be like you are? Why should you blame him for allowing Satan to rebel, when he allowed you to? The answer is very simple, God is a Father, and he does not force any of his creatures to go his way. He gives you freedom to rebel. We cannot grumble about him giving the angels freedom, though they have superior intelligence and strength, because he gave us the same freedom, and we have used it in the wrong way. So that is what kind of a person he is.

Satan has a special power and interest in the earth, out of the whole of space. The Bible gives no indication that Lucifer, star of the morning who fell from his place in heaven, has control over any more than earth and its atmosphere. Sometimes he is called the prince of the power of the air. So whenever I pray, between me and the heavenlies, there is the air, and I am praying right through the territory of a prince of darkness whose avowed intention is to establish on earth a kingdom of disease, a kingdom of death, a kingdom of darkness in which he has the final word.

Among Christians I find two extremes. There are those who joke about Satan, which is a big mistake. Read *The Screwtape Letters*, but not as a comedy, read it as a tragedy, because it is a tragic book. It is a marvellous book if you want to understand Satan, but do not laugh at it. Laugh at yourself, but not at Satan. Some other Christians have another funny attitude to him: they blame him for everything that goes wrong, and make him a scapegoat. But I do not believe he is responsible for all that goes wrong in my life. I think vividly of a man who told me that he forgot to set his alarm clock. He got up late, he rushed his breakfast, got indigestion, ran for the station, got to the station just as the train was running out, arrived at his office and was torn off a strip for being late, and he tore a strip off somebody else further down the line. He came back home, and at the fellowship meeting that night he said, 'The devil has been having a real go at me today.' I do not believe the devil was involved at any stage in that process. He forgot to set his alarm clock! There are three sources of temptation: the world, the flesh and the devil, and you cannot blame it all on the devil. We need some straight thinking here. But I tell you that if some people take him too lightly and some people blame him too easily, the true Christian takes the devil very seriously indeed. I just hope that you never have a direct encounter with him, because it is pretty scary; and you can only come through it because you know that he is already a defeated foe.

Did you know that there are two books in the Bible that the devil hates more than any other, out of all sixty-six? There are two that say more about him than any others and it is these that he has attacked more than the rest. They are the one at the beginning and the one at the end: Genesis and Revelation. And do you know why he hates them? Because Genesis describes his devices, and Revelation describes his doom. And there has been more scholarly attack on the book of Genesis than any other book, and more attempt to turn it into myth and legend and away from fact than any other book in the Bible. Why? Because Satan does not want you to believe that Genesis chapter 3 ever happened. He does not want you to know how he got hold of Eve, he does not want you to believe that he said what he did to that first married couple. Satan attacks the book of Genesis.

But the other book which he hates more than any other is Revelation, because as you read that book you come to a point where it tells how the devil himself will be cast into that lake of fire. He will be bound in prison first, and not allowed to trouble men —and then, finally, he will be put in the lake of fire. He so hates that bit, and I am going to tell you something now that may make you a little scared. When I preach through the book of Revelation there are more disturbances and things go wrong in the congregation than in any other series I ever take. On one occasion I came to that chapter, and I preached my way through it, and a tape was made of my talk. A short while later, about forty miles from my church, on the south coast of England, one of that series of tapes went to a family of new Christians. The wife had been a Christian for about six months, the husband and their teenager had just come to the Lord, and they were building themselves up, listening to these tapes. They listened to Revelation, and they came to the tape which described the downfall of Satan. They were sitting in an ordinary sitting room listening, and when I began to mention Satan, over on the tape, on top of my voice and blotting it out, there was a shrieking foreign tongue. They could hear my voice in the background, but they could not make out one word of what I said. They were scared, and they sent for a minister whom I know, and he went to them. They said, 'This is what happened — for about seven minutes we couldn't hear a word of what Mr Pawson was saying.'

So he said, 'Well, play it through for me again.' They played it through a second time, and this time there was not one sound for seven minutes. Now you can understand a little better who I am talking about. It is as serious as that. He hates people talking about him in truth and warning people about his intentions. So take him seriously.

But I must tell you that the Bible makes it

absolutely clear that Satan is already a defeated foe, and if he gets hold of you he is bluffing you. Call his bluff. If you have been baptised, say, 'Satan, I'm not only dead, I'm buried. You are talking to a dead man.' Don't you know that in baptism you are buried with Christ? That is the point of baptism: to have a funeral of someone who has died, and the funeral helps you to say goodbye to an old life. It says: that is finished; that is the last time I see that life. Satan does not like people getting baptised, for that reason. He does not like us having a public funeral of someone who has died. Because when you reckon yourself dead, and call his bluff and say, 'I am dead and buried, and Satan you saw my funeral, you were present there and know that I am dead and buried, stop tempting me', you will find, to your extraordinary delight, that he has to go. *Resist the devil and he will run from you* — and you resist him on the ground of fact and on the ground of the word of God.

Let us now think about his relationship to prayer. Since Jesus came and died and rose again and returned to glory, Satan's work on earth is to destroy everything that Jesus builds, if he possibly can. That is why I warn everyone I baptise, expect the devil to try to rob you of that blessing in some subtle way soon. That is what he tried to do with Jesus. What was the blessing that Jesus had in his baptism? The blessing Jesus had was an assurance of his sonship. *'You are my beloved Son.'* So what did the devil say to him within six weeks? The devil said, *'If you are the Son of God . . .'* and he tried to sow the seed of doubt about the very assurance that he had. So he is trying to destroy everything that Jesus is building.

We now need to consider two issues. The first is a rather negative one: what the devil can do to us in prayer; the second is a more positive one: what we can do to him in prayer.

Let us start with what he can do to us in prayer. If he is the prince of the power of the air, wherever I am in the atmosphere of earth, when I pray, then his territory lies between me and heaven, as I have already said, and I have to break through enemy territory to communicate. That is my problem.

So the two things the devil will try to do are: to stop me praying and, if I manage to start, to spoil it. But we are not ignorant of his tricks — thank

God the Bible makes it clear. How does he stop my prayer? Well, depending on my temperament, he attacks one of the three parts of my personality. I have a heart, a mind and a will, and depending on my temperament, he attacks one of these three points. He attacks my will — my will to pray. He can do it through my laziness. Who said that prayer was the power of mind over mattress? Have you heard that definition? If he does not use laziness then he can use busyness, and get your will so involved in other things. Supposing you are not the type whose will can be attacked, then he can attack your mind and fill your mind with questions as to whether prayer really works — with philosophical arguments. One doctrine the devil just loves to use as an argument against prayer is the doctrine of predestination. He says it is all fixed anyway; God has made his decisions and prayer cannot do anything about it except line up with what God has already decided. Do not believe it, prayer can even change God's mind. So the devil fills your mind with doubts about the efficacy of prayer.

If you are the sort of person who is more

emotional then he can play havoc with your feelings in relation to prayer. He can say, 'You don't
feel anything do you? So nothing is happening.'
Or he can take the affections of your heart, and so
plant them on someone else, and so direct them
to someone else, that you have no affection left for
God in prayer. He can take a young man and so
concentrate all his affection on a young lady that
the young man has no affection left for the Lord,
and his heart is robbed from God. I do not know
which way he gets at you most, but he will get at
you either with your will, and make it weak, or in
your mind, and get it confused, or in your heart,
and get it hollow and empty of feeling for the Lord.
Whichever way he does it, he has stopped you
praying. Therefore, I honestly believe that the most
valuable prayer is when you do not feel like it, or
when you are having a battle to do it, or when your
mind is as confused as Job's, but you are going to
go on talking to God.

Now how does Satan try to spoil your prayer
once you have started? I think I can sum it up
like this: he tries to get you unbalanced in your
prayer. With some people that means he tries to

get you just endlessly praying and thinking that somehow the length of your prayer is going to change heaven; with other people he tries to get them all on praise and not on asking; with others, all on asking and not on thanking; with others, all on thanking and not on confession. He will try to get it out of balance.

I had a discussion with someone who said he thought there was no place for set prayers, no place for prayers out of a book, no place for using a form of words, it all had to be spontaneous. 'Indeed,' he said, 'if it is all in tongues it is better still.' Now that is an unbalanced way, and the devil wants to unbalance your prayer. He does not like people such as Paul, who say: I will pray with the mind and I will pray in the Spirit; I am going to do both. You find in the New Testament that not only did they have extemporary, spontaneous prayer, it says they *continued steadfastly in the apostles' doctrine, the breaking of bread, the fellowship and THE prayers* — which were the liturgical prayers.

There is nothing wrong with prayers from a book if the prayer is inspired by the Holy Spirit. The devil likes to get you unbalanced, so that you are limited to one kind of prayer only. 'Unless it is extemporary prayer it is not real prayer.' Have you heard that? 'Prayer out of a book is not real prayer.' Sometimes when you are not having too good a time with your own prayer life, a very good thing to do is to get hold of a book of prayer, and use somebody else's for a time, and freshen up with their communion. Let the Spirit teach you from the way they pray. Why not? You don't mind singing a hymn from a book, do you? Study the temptations of our Lord, and you will find how he met the devil in prayer, how he was able to stop the devil driving a wedge between him and his heavenly Father, again and again. He used the Bible particularly — three times he threw the book at the devil.

So here are the two things that the devil will try to do: he will try to stop you praying through your heart, mind and will; he will try and spoil your prayer by getting it unbalanced and getting you into only one kind of prayer, or one aspect of prayer, so that in fact it will go stale because it is not varied enough. Soon it will be either ritualism or 'rutualism' —and it is hard to know which is worse.

Let us turn to the positive side: what we can do to the devil in prayer. This is exciting. We can lay him flat in prayer. We are told in the New Testament that we are to take the initiative against him. Do you know that Jesus told us to pray every day about the devil? We find this in the prayer that he taught his disciples when they said, *'Lord, teach us to pray.'* He said that they were to pray like this —'Dad in heaven', then to pray for the things he wants: his name to be hallowed, his kingdom to come, his will to be done on earth as in heaven. Then they were to pray for the things they needed —food; forgiveness. Then he told them to finish by praying this: *'Deliver us from the evil ONE.'* Some English translations do not convey that. In our thinking we have turned evil into a thing, but evil is not a thing, it is a person. There is no evil anywhere in the universe apart from persons. (And there is no love in the universe apart from persons who love.) Evil is an intensely personal thing so Jesus told disciples to pray daily, *'Deliver us from the evil one.'* Start your prayer by thinking of your Dad in heaven, but end your prayer by thinking of the devil on earth, and go out to face him. We can be delivered, through prayer, from the power of the evil one.

There are three things that the devil can do to people, according to the Bible, and prayer can deliver them from all three. Firstly, he can bind their bodies in sickness. That does not mean that all sickness is from Satan, nor that God removes all sickness in answer to prayer. Even if sickness is from Satan, God does not always remove it. The classic case of that is 2 Corinthians 12, where Paul says he had a 'thorn in the flesh'. I believe that in its simplest, straightforward meaning, this meant a physical handicap. Three times he prayed that God would remove this messenger of Satan from his body, and God said no — he would keep Paul humble so that people can see grace is sufficient. That is not a reason for leaving everyone in that condition, only Paul in that case. A woman had come to Jesus with a particular complaint. Did his disciples really see her? Did they see what the matter with her was — that she was a prisoner? That Satan had bound her physically for eighteen years? Jesus saw this and set her free. That puts the other side.

Satan can bind bodies. One of the things that he did to my fellowship at one time was to give sickness to one person after another to try and stop the work. In the name of Jesus, I declared then and continue to declare today that he is not winning, he is losing, but he is still fighting in this way.

If prayer can deliver from Satan, from the evil one, then it is right to pray for the sick. It is right to ask Jesus if he will sign a petition for health for a brother or sister in the Lord.

The second thing that Satan can do is to blind people's minds. The god of this world has blinded their minds so they cannot see, says the Scripture. I have met some pretty intelligent people in my time – scholars, professors, people with an IQ way above mine – and the incredible thing to me is this: they seem able to master every subject but the simple truth about God. Have you met people like this? They are clever, but you talk to them about God and they cannot see it. Lord, I thank you that you have hidden it from men like that and given it to babes and sucklings, because if heaven is for high IQs, most of us are finished! We can pray, 'Deliver us from the evil one', then we can pray that even brilliant intellects can have their blindness taken away.

So Satan binds men's bodies and prayer can deliver a man from Satan physically. He can blind a mind, and you can set a man free from a blinded mind through prayer. What else does Satan do? He can capture the spirits of men too, and he can get them locked up in a religion that will keep them from God. That may sound extraordinary, but the greatest enemy of Christianity is religion – including the religion of England called 'churchianity' – and other religions. What is the greatest problem that missionaries encounter? It is the religion which people already have. Satan knows that man is a religious being. He knows that man prays, that there is a God-shaped blank in the human soul; and he knows that if he leaves that blank, people will look for God, they will seek God. Happily, they may find him. So what does Satan do? He fills the blank with religion. All kinds of new religions have appeared, and more are appearing on the horizon.

Satan wants to capture men in their bodies and bind them to him in disease; he wants to capture their minds and blind them with confusion and doubt; he wants to capture men's spirits and bind them to him in religion. If there is one thing that a Christian rejoices in, it is that he has been saved from religion. Do you rejoice in that? When people talk to you about 'religion', do you feel awkward and not know quite what to say? You might say, 'Well, I'm not religious — I'm a Christian!'

Satan is very happy if people have religion. But by prayer we can bind the strong man and spoil his goods. That is how Jesus talked about Satan. He taught like this: When I set this person free from disease or a demon possession or anything else, what am I doing? I am binding a strong man and spoiling his goods. But he said that you have to bind the strong man first. You do not burgle a strong man's house until you have him tied up. The glorious thing is that by the blood of Jesus you can bind Satan, then you can spoil his goods. *'Lead us not into temptation, but deliver us from the evil one.'*

I have said that prayer is a battle. It is to get into the front line, but Paul would say that it is to get into the ring. He would say that prayer is wrestling — not that you are shooting at Satan from a distance. You get so close to Satan, to the powers of evil, that there are times when it feels like hand-to-hand wrestling. That is very close. There are times when evil feels so real that you could just touch it, you can almost smell it.

How are you going to win that battle? I think the answer is that there is a proper dress for wrestlers. What should a Christian wear when he prays? Have you ever thought about that one? I do not recommend a dressing gown and slippers! I recommend the whole armour of God. That is what you will need — and that means the whole armour, not just bits of it. The problem is that if you leave one piece of armour off that is where the enemy will attack. That is what happens in wrestling, boxing, and indeed any form of fighting at close quarters: your opponent is looking for the one weak point, the one gap in your defence. So Paul, writing about praying, says that you need the whole armour of God, and you will need every bit of it. Miss one bit out and that is where you will lose the battle. Do pay attention to that. You need the truth. Tie yourself tightly!

My father, when he was a boy, worked on a farm, as I did. I remember him telling me about a big, burly Irishman who worked on the farm, and whenever he was really going to get down to lifting a heavy sack he had a great wide leather belt and he would pull it up two notches before he bent down for the sack. When he pulled his belt in, he was ready, he was held together; he would then bend down, and up would come the sack. Paul says: when you are going to pray, pull your belt in with truth. Make sure you are held together with truth. He did not say make sure your feelings are right, or that the mood is right, he said get truth right. Pull yourself together with truth. Then he said, cover your heart with righteousness, because if there is one thing that makes prayer difficult it is a guilty conscience. Get that right. Cover your heart with the breastplate of righteousness, and then your conscience will not condemn you as you pray. Then he says your feet need to be ready to run somewhere with the gospel if you are going to pray properly. Your feet need to be shod with the gospel of peace. Are you ready to go and take that gospel to someone else after you have prayed?

Right, then your feet are all right, and Satan will not lead them in the wrong way. What about your arms? You need a shield and you will need to move it. There will be fiery darts coming. That was one of the favourite weapons in the old days: an arrow soaked in pitch and set alight was a deadly thing. So the Roman soldier had a big, heavy shield that was quite thick and made of soft wood, and the arrow came into it and burned out in the soft wood. Paul said that you will need the shield of faith. Do you really believe that God is listening? You will need that shield. Then Paul reminds us about protecting the head. Do you have problems with wandering thoughts? Of course you do. I have told you one way to get over that, and it is to say your prayers out loud rather than to think them. But the best protection against wandering thoughts is to fill your head with thoughts of salvation; put on the helmet of salvation; get your head full of salvation. You could start your prayer, maybe, by saying, 'God you have saved me. I'm going to think about that.' That is a good thought that will not wander.

Have you noticed that so far all this is defence? But we are not going to be on the defensive with the devil, we want to attack too, so you will need one more thing: a sword — the 'sword of the Spirit'. Now a sword is pushed through the belt of truth, and some people think the sword of the Spirit is the whole Bible, but that is not the case. The belt is the Bible, for the belt is the truth. The sword which you pull from it is the word which the Spirit pulls from that truth in that situation. Each time Jesus answered the devil, he pulled a different sword out from his belt and he attacked.

Do not let the devil have it all his own way. Put on the whole armour and you have that weapon of attack, the right word from God's word which the Spirit enables you to give from the truth; it may be a word from the Bible, it may be a word direct from the Spirit that is not in the Bible, but it is a word that the Spirit will give you, a word from God, and you attack the devil with that. Say, 'Shut up and run away' —and you will find he does.

You will be defended in that day, and you will be able to attack. It is total warfare. That is why prayer is a much harder thing for Christians than for others, because the devil hates prayer from Christians — far more than all the Tibetan prayer wheels and the Muslim prayer mats. He hates the name of Jesus because Jesus – the name high over all in hell or earth or sky – angels and men before it fall, and devils fear and fly. Do you believe that? Then pray that the blood of Jesus may not only protect the work that is going on already, but enlarge it to the glory of God. Pray against Satan, who is attacking members of fellowships even now and trying to lay them low; who is trying to confuse people's minds; who is trying to give them religion instead of a relationship with Christ, and let us pray: Lord, deliver us from the evil one. For thine is the kingdom – not his – thine is the power, and thine is the glory, for ever and ever. *Amen.*

PRAYER

Thank you, Lord, for keeping the devil at bay this day. We pray now, in the name of Jesus, that those whom he is troubling at this very moment will be delivered and given the freedom of the sons of God in body, mind and spirit. Lord, we did not become aware of how much hold he had on us until we came to know you, then we realised how powerful, subtle and intelligent he is. But, Lord, we thank you that he is no match for Jesus, and that he overreached himself at the cross. Lord, give us the victory, we pray, not for our sake but the sake of your holy name. May the prayers of our churches be more powerful than the prince of this world and all his principalities, for we ask it in the name of Jesus, our Lord and Saviour. *Amen.*

5

PRAYER WITH THE SAINTS

*While they were talking to the people, the priests,
the captain of the temple police and some of the
Sadducees came over to them, very disturbed that
Peter and John were claiming that Jesus had risen
from the dead. They arrested them, and since it was
already evening, put them in prison for the night.
But many of the people who heard their message
believed it, so that the number of believers now
reached a new peak of about five thousand men.
The next day it happened that a council of all the
Jewish leaders was in session in Jerusalem. Ananias,
the high priest, was there and Caiaphas, John,
Alexander, and others of the high priest's relatives.
So the two disciples were brought in before them.
'By what power or by whose authority have you done
this?' the council demanded.*

Then Peter, filled with the Holy Spirit, said to them: 'Honourable leaders and elders of our nation, if you mean the good deed done to the cripple and how he was healed, let me clearly state to you and to all the people of Israel that it was done in the name and power of Jesus from Nazareth, the Messiah whom you crucified but whom God brought back to life again. It is by his authority that this man stands here healed, for Jesus the Messiah is the one referred to in the Scriptures when they speak of a stone discarded by the builders which became the capstone of the arch. There is salvation in no-one else; under all heaven there is no other name for men to call upon and save them.'

When the council saw the boldness of Peter and John and could see that they were obviously uneducated working men, they were amazed and realised what being with Jesus had done for them. And the council could hardly discredit the healing when the man they had healed was standing right there beside them. So they sent them out of the council chamber and conferred among themselves. 'What shall we do with these men?' they asked each other. 'We can't deny that they have done a tremendous miracle, and everybody in Jerusalem knows about it. But perhaps we can stop them spreading their propaganda. We'll tell them that if they do it again we'll really throw the book at them.' So they called them back in and told them never again to speak about Jesus.

But Peter and John replied, 'You decide whether God wants us to obey you instead of him. We cannot stop telling about the wonderful things that we saw Jesus do and heard him say.' The council then threatened them further and finally let them go because they did not know how to punish them without starting a riot, for everyone was praising God for this wonderful miracle, the healing of a man who had been lame for forty years.

As soon as they were free, Peter and John found the other disciples and told them what the council had said, then all the believers united in this prayer:

'O Lord, Creator of heaven and earth and of the sea and everything in them, you spoke long ago by the Holy Spirit through our ancestor King David, your servant, saying, "Why do the heathen rage against the Lord, and the foolish nations plan their little plots against Almighty God?" The kings of the earth unite

to fight against him, against the anointed Son of God. That is what is happening here in this city today, for Herod the king, and Pontius Pilate the governor, and all the Romans, as well as the people of Israel, are united against Jesus, your anointed Son, your holy servant. They won't stop at anything that you and your wise power will let them do. And now, O Lord, hear their threats and grant to your servants great boldness in their preaching, and send your healing power, and may miracles and wonders be done by the name of your holy servant Jesus.'

After this prayer, the building where they were meeting shook, and they were all filled with the Holy Spirit and boldly preached God's message. All the believers were of one heart and mind, and no-one felt that what he owned was his own. Everything was shared, and the apostles preached powerful sermons about the resurrection of the Lord Jesus, and there was warm fellowship among all the believers, and no poverty, for all who owned land or houses sold them and brought the money to the apostles for others in need.

(Acts 4)

That is exciting, and you just want to go on reading and reading! Those events need not be as days in the past.

Looking along my bookshelves at the books on this subject of prayer, I noticed how many of them included the word 'private' in their title. Leslie Weatherhead produced *A Private House of Prayer* and there was a very famous book by John Baillie, *A Diary of Private Prayer*. Without wanting to quibble with that, I would repeat what I wrote above, that there is no such thing as private prayer for the Christian, and in Christian thinking the very minimum for prayer is four persons. As a Christian you cannot possibly pray without at least four — Father, Son, Spirit and yourself. But I am afraid others will try to get in on the act pretty quickly. We have looked at the intervention of the devil, who will try to invade that situation, and he can bring with him principalities and powers, but I believe that angels get involved too, and you pray with angels, archangels and all the company of heaven. But I particularly want to think about the dimension of praying with the saints. I do not believe you can pray without them. As I mentioned earlier, Jesus said, if you are going to have some secret prayer, go into a room, shut the door, get all alone and then pray. That meant *with the saints* because you are to pray like this: '*Our* Father, which art in heaven, hallowed be thy name; give *us* this day our daily bread' — even though yours is the only body in that room! You are praying with the saints. In other words, once you become a Christian you cease to be an individual, you become a member of the body, and it is the body that prays, even when you are on your own. It is the other religions that talk about private prayer. It is the other religions that think you only need two people for prayer — yourself and God. In the Bible, corporate prayer *is* prayer, and even if your body is on its own, all prayer is corporate prayer; it is the prayer of all the saints.

Now this comes out in what Jesus did. So often, even when he prayed very personally to his Father, he was not alone. Think for a moment about Luke 9:18, which tells us that as Jesus was praying alone his disciples were with him! When he wanted to pray privately and personally, he would take Peter and James and John with him, just for support. It is extraordinary how often that happens. I suppose the prayer of Jesus is John 17 – the prayer he prayed with his Father the night before he died – and that was a very intimate and a terribly personal prayer. *'Father, I thank you for the glory I had with you before the world was, and I thank you that you are going to give it back to me.'* And *I* thank you for this and *I* thank you for that . . . . But where did he pray it? He prayed it with the saints; he prayed it in the presence of all his disciples. Later, in Gethsemane, when he was going to battle through with the biggest battle of his life, he asked the disciples to stay awake — to watch and pray. It is as though he were saying that he wanted to be with the saints, to be surrounded — wanting help and support. If Jesus needed that, then so do you, and prayer with the saints is vital. Think about what he did as well as what he said.

Prayer is always corporate prayer. Bear in mind that whenever you start talking to the Father you are joining thousands of others. If you pray out loud at the same time as others, God still hears every prayer quite distinctly. We are joining with all the saints.

I want to look at this matter of praying with the saints, very briefly and very simply from four angles. Firstly, I want to look at the biblical basis for praying together; secondly, at the added advantages of praying together; thirdly, at the practical problems of praying together (and I am very much aware of those, as you may be); and, fourthly, at what I want to call the 'concentric circles' of praying together.

First, we look at the biblical basis and I take simply the New Testament. There are four parts of the New Testament that I want to refer to here: the Gospels, Acts, the Epistles, and Revelation. Did you know that in each of these there is more about praying together than there is about praying alone? The promises in the Gospels are nearly all made to people praying together rather than praying alone. The practice in Acts is nearly always praying together rather than praying alone. The precepts in the Epistles are nearly always praying together. Finally, the predictions in the book of Revelation are about people praying together. That puts it in a pretty important light.

Take first the promises in the Gospels. Here is

one, for example. Jesus said, *'I say to you if two of you agree on earth about anything they ask, it will be done for them by my Father in heaven, for where two or three are gathered in my name, there am I in the midst of them.'* That is a promise you cannot claim unless you pray with one or two others. It is a promise you have to leave on one side if you always pray alone, and it is a promise of the Lord Jesus.

But when I went through John's Gospel chapters 14, 15 and 16, I discovered something important for our understanding. It was the night before Jesus died, when he gave the disciples more instruction about prayer than perhaps at any other time. He wanted to teach them how to keep in touch with the Father when he was away from them.

They had 'lived with' the Father for three years, for Jesus said, *'If you have seen me you have seen the Father.'* He was leaving them and he wanted them to learn to keep in touch with God, so he made many specific promises to them — and each promise included the phrase 'in my name' — *'whatever you ask in my name, I will do it for you.'* But when I read that in the Greek, I learned something more. In the English we only have one word 'you' for singular and plural, so we do not know when we read the English Bible which Jesus actually used, but in the Greek you do know, and in every case in these promises about prayer the word 'you' is in the plural, not the singular. He is not saying 'when each of you or any of you asks in my name', he is saying 'when you together ask in my name'. That throws a different light on things, doesn't it? When you *together* — it is all of a piece with 'when two or three are gathered together'. There is something special about prayer together. Three people praying separately cannot achieve what three people praying together can achieve, according to these promises.

Move on to the practice in Acts. What were they doing in the ten days between the ascension of our Lord and the Day of Pentecost? They were praying, but how were they praying? Were they each off in some bedroom, saying, 'Lord, fill me with your Holy Spirit'? Nothing of the kind. They were all together saying, 'Lord, fill us with your Holy Spirit' — and there is more power in prayer for the Holy Spirit together than alone. Too many people are seeking to be filled privately. They would much rather it would happen privately, in a sense, because then it might not be so embarrassing. There is power in a group together. Get 120 people together praying until the Lord fills them all with the Holy Spirit, and something will happen. In Acts chapter 1 they were not all praying separately to be filled, they were together. Mary the virgin was there; she did not know that she was going to be filled and speak in other tongues, but she did. The Holy Spirit came on her a second time, but this time she was part of a body of people who were praying.

Then, in Acts chapter 2, they got three thousand converts. If you can get 120 people praying together daily, you are going to see something happen! Now notice what took place. After they baptised the converts, they then taught them how to go on in the Christian life. And what did they teach them? They taught them to come together to listen to teaching, they taught them to come together for fellowship, they taught them to come together for breaking of bread, and they taught them to come together for prayer — from the very beginning. That is intriguing. Turn the pages and we find some lovely accounts of prayer meetings. There was the one mentioned in Acts chapter 4. They had been told to never again mention the name of Jesus, so they got together for a prayer meeting, and you know what they prayed. They said, 'Lord, help us to speak boldly in the name of Jesus.' They did not say, 'Lord, keep us quiet', or, 'Lord, keep us under control'. They got together, and you can pray for boldness when you are together. It is when you are alone that Satan can pick you off one by one, but when you are together praying for boldness to speak, you get it. The very fact of being together in prayer for courage is support. Indeed, I believe that there should be a minimum of two Christians in every place. It is the single Christians who are weak. You need at least two of you together in your office; if you are the only one, then pray that God will send someone else to be with you, so that at least there are two of you to pray. If one can chase a thousand, two can put ten thousand to flight. I can never explain God's mathematics, but somehow it works!

Then, in chapter eight, again you find praying for the Holy Ghost to come in power, and it is *together*

—they are not praying privately or separately, they are praying together. Or turn to Acts 12, which I think is the funniest prayer meeting there has ever been. Somebody was in prison. It was Peter, and they were all having a prayer meeting for him, and while they were praying there was a knock on the door. A young lady got up from her seat, went to answer it, and told them that it was Peter. They said, 'It can't be, we're praying for him and he's in prison.' Now you can make of that what you like, but I make of it lack of faith. They just could not believe that their prayer was answered as promptly as that with a knock on the door. But they were praying together about those in prison, and we too can pray together for those in prison. Turn the pages and you find that it was when a group of people were praying together that God called missionaries, and I tell you this: every church that is sending missionaries overseas is a church that is praying together. Where churches pray together, God will separate people for particular tasks.

Now turn to the Epistles. Have you ever counted up, when you read Paul's letters, how many times he asks his readers to pray? But did you know that every time he does so he uses the word 'you' in the plural, and he always says something that implies he does not just want them to remember him in private prayer, he wants them to get together and pray for him? It comes out even more clearly in the Greek than the English.

Finally, turn to the predictions in the book of Revelation. The last days are going to be very difficult for the church of Christ. They are going to be under pressure; Antichrist will reign; there will be real persecution. What is going to be the defence of the church against those tough times coming? It will be the incense of the prayers of the saints. The incense rises from saints gathered together in the book of Revelation. They are praying together and upholding each other in prayer. There is security in their prayer together; they are supporting each other as they face the opposition of the enemy. The enemy loves to get us separately and pick us off one by one.

This gives you the biblical basis. There is much in the New Testament about praying alone, but there is far more about praying together.

Now let us look at the added advantages. What

can united prayer do that separate prayer cannot — apart, that is, from the promise of Christ that he will be there in the midst if two or three are gathered in his name?

I have found three advantages:

1. It turns prayer into a school.

2. It turns prayer into a fireplace.

3. It turns prayer into a powerhouse.

It turns prayer into a school. I have learned more about prayer from listening to other people pray than from all the books on prayer on my shelves, and from all the sermons that I have heard about prayer. There is nothing like listening to other people pray to learn how to pray. It really does stimulate you in prayer, it opens up new possibilities to you, and you think: I never thought of praying for that, or like that. It makes you want to expand your own prayer. So I praise God for groups where I have been able to listen to the saints pray. Somehow, seeing it done by the saints corrects your own prayers. You stop praying for such selfish things, you begin to get a bigger vision, you pray for bigger things, and it saves you from the kind of rut you were in, because the variety of personality enriches your own understanding of prayer.

Secondly, praying together turns prayer into a 'fireplace'. What do I mean by that? You take out of the fire a piece of coal that is burning brightly and put it on the hearth by itself, then see what happens to it. Its potential to be hot does not change, but it does go cool. It still has all the fuel within in it to burn, yet it goes cool. Immediately you put it back in among the other coals, it warms up again. Martin Luther wrote in his diary, 'At home in my own house there is no warmth or vigour in me, but in the church, when the multitude is gathered together, a fire is kindled in my heart and it breaks its way through.' That was a very honest thing for the great reformer to say. He was saying: I need to be in the fireplace. There is no doubt that if you are cool in your private prayer, if you are finding it tough going, you need to get into the fireplace, get in among some hot coals, and the glow can be communicated and taken back into your own prayer life.

So first it is a school in which you learn more from listening to others, second it is a fireplace in which you catch the glow and begin to get warmed up yourself, and thirdly it is a powerhouse.

Whenever I dare to venture out of my own sphere, an expert in that field appears! But, as I understand it, a cable which is going to carry electricity is made up of smaller wires bundled together. Together those wires can carry far more power than they could separately. You look at the flex next time you put it into a plug, and it is made up of a lot of little strands. Those strands together can carry a lot of power, and it just seems that God has so ordained prayer that if you put a lot of little strands together, the power that can be carried is so much greater because you are together. Do not ask me how it works, but it seems to be another case of what Henry Drummond referred to as natural law in the spiritual world.

Many years ago there was a church in Shanghai which had only sixty members, and they just stayed level, nothing seemed to be happening.

So what did they do? They divided their sixty members into ten groups of six. Some people would say, 'That is mechanical, you are trying to do the work of the Spirit for him.' Well, I would rather be in the Shanghai church, from what I am going to tell you now. They assumed that every member was ready to pray with others — that is quite an assumption, but they made it. They said that since that is a normal part of New Testament Christianity, it is a contradiction in terms to have a church member who does not join in a prayer meeting. They gave them each one hour of the working day to pray. How they organised it with their work, I do not know. I think they were mostly self-employed, or workers on the land who could arrange their own work. One group of six prayed from eight until nine in the morning, then from nine to ten, and so on, right through the day, until during every day and night there was continuous prayer in groups of six. The first year – from the day they started doing this – they had one hundred and fourteen baptisms, and in the second year they had two hundred baptisms. The only change that they had made in the situation was that they were now praying together, not in a big church prayer meeting but in groups of six, and that is what did the trick. Intriguing! Dare I say — try it! There is a need to increase the percentage of Christians in this country. You can change public opinion, and therefore public trends, when you have five per cent of the population. How are we going to do that? It would not take so long if we did what that church in Shanghai did. I am throwing that out as a challenge to you.

While I was in Canada, I met Dr Donald McGavran, an upright little man with a brilliant brain, who devoted part of his life to studying books and writing about one topic only — how churches grow. He has been all over the world, analysing, examining, questioning, observing, asking how churches grow, and he has produced a lot of literature. He has not given over-simplistic answers. He said there are different factors operating (some have a big evangelist, some have good buildings, and so on), but there is only one common factor which applies to every church throughout the world that is growing rapidly: they are churches with groups of Christians meeting together regularly to pray for non-Christians by name, in the name of Jesus. You cannot do that in a big crowd, you cannot do it in a public space, but you can do it in a group where two or three are gathered together.

Thirdly, I want to address the practical problems of praying together, and there are some. I have six in mind, and I am sure that you could add to them. I nearly listed six types of people who are problems in prayer together, but that would be naughty! We will just label them problems, not people, and if the cap fits we can all wear it.

First, there is the problem of those who remain silent. When we come together to pray, everybody should be ready to pray, and to be silent can in fact hinder a prayer meeting. It is very rarely that the problem is physical. I know a man who has the worst stammer of anybody I have ever met. If you say, 'Good morning' to him, he staggers over the 'G' before he can reply 'Good morning'. But the Lord took hold of him, and when he goes to a prayer meeting the Lord gives him such a fluency that it pours out – the only time that he is free from the stammer – isn't that lovely? The Lord has not healed him of his stammer in talking to people, but the Lord so wants people to talk to him, and to talk to him in a prayer meeting, that he releases him from that stammer and it pours out — and I have never heard such a man of prayer.

No, the barrier is far more often psychological. We may be so overcome with nerves, fright, fear, self-consciousness, that there is a blockage, and like Pharaoh we have a plague of frogs in our throats! We think, 'If I start, how am I going to stop?' Or, 'What if I can't continue?' Or, 'What if I get stuck, if my mind goes blank? — and in any case there are people here who can pray much better than I can, and they'll be comparing their prayer with mine, and they'll be thinking about me all the time; they'll think "Ah, so he's like that, is he?"' So we close up.

My grandfather, who was a minister, went out to lunch one Sunday. It was clear that it was a home where they never said grace before a meal, but because he was wearing a dog collar the wife said brightly to the husband, 'Will you say grace, darling?' He looked quite shattered! He started, he went through Psalm 23, the Lord's Prayer and he went on and on and on, every little bit of a Collect he could remember, and he simply did not know how to finish. My grandfather, who had quite a sense of humour, suddenly came out with a loud 'Amen', and that finished the prayer! The poor man had just been embarrassed!

When someone who has been silent utters a prayer, however simple and brief it is, I often find that prayer by far the most helpful. It is so real — when they get over that psychological barrier. A woman came to me once, saying, 'I'll make tea at the church, I'll scrub the floors, I'll do anything, but don't ask me to pray in a prayer meeting.'

I said, 'Look, would you really like to? That is the key question to me, not whether you can but would you wish to?'

After looking at me for a long time, she answered, 'Yes, I would like to, I wish I could.'

I said, 'Right, will you put yourself in my hands for six weeks?'

She replied, 'Yes, I will.'

I told her that the next prayer meeting was next week and said, 'I want you to go home, and I want you to get a little piece of paper and a pencil, and I want you to write out a prayer of not more than one sentence, and write *Amen* at the end of it. I want you to come next week and at the prayer meeting, when your turn comes, just read that sentence, no more.' She did that; it was a lovely little prayer, so she got the sentence out, and then she choked up just after the word 'amen'. The next week I said, 'For this time I want you to write out another sentence prayer, but now I want you to memorise the sentence.' Then, step by step, we got her over the psychological hurdles of hearing her own voice in public managing to finish, and so on. Within six weeks she was praying and loving it. The Lord wants to deal with your psychological barriers because he wants you to pray, he wants you to be able to take part. He does not want you to have an inferiority complex.

But I believe there are also other reasons why people are silent in a prayer meeting. There may be spiritual reasons. I have noticed that people who carry bitterness or resentment in their heart tend to go quiet at a prayer meeting. They need to deal with those things before they can be free to pray. They need to get rid of them. Robert Louis Stevenson had the practice of saying the Lord's

Prayer at his breakfast table with his family each day, just the Lord's Prayer. One day he began, 'Our Father . . .' and then he stopped, got up, and ran out into the kitchen.

His wife went out to him and said, 'Are you all right?' and he said he was. 'Well,' she said, 'why didn't you pray it through?'

He replied, 'I'm not fit to', and she asked why not. 'Because,' he said, 'there is someone I can't forgive.' That is honesty. If the silence is due to that kind of thing, then we have to get it dealt with and take it to the Lord. You may be angry or quarrelsome, or have something spiritual in your heart that is keeping you quiet. 1 Timothy 2:8 says that you must have pure intentions when you come to prayer.

The second problem is a practical one: those who are inaudible. Some people seem to pray to their shoes! If you are going to pray together, then out of love for the others present you must lift your head and lift your voice. Speak up, and ensure that the others present can hear (rather than keeping your voice to the level you use when you are praying alone) so that they can share your prayer.

The third problem is that of lengthy prayers. The amount of time a congregation, or even a prayer meeting, can concentrate on one person praying is very limited. Somebody has reckoned that a typical congregation cannot concentrate for more than one minute. I do not know what research they did for that – I know some that can continue much longer – but what they were saying is that after one minute in a public service the first person will begin to wander away in thought, and will soon be followed by others. The compilers of the Book of Common Prayer realised this and produced common prayers deliberately for people to share in common, and such a 'common prayer' does not usually last much more than a minute. There was a very sound principle for that. They knew that it is better to have many short prayers than one long one. The trouble is that in reacting against the political imposition by the government of a Book of Common Prayer, the free churches reacted against both brief prayers and book prayers, and I think that is sad. There are treasuries, riches of prayer in books, that we may miss. We have long extemporary prayers, and think they are more spiritual than those short Collects from the Book of Common Prayer, some of which are so brief yet so deep. 'Almighty God, unto whom all hearts be open, all desires known, and from whom no secrets are hid; Cleanse the thoughts of our hearts by the inspiration of thy Holy Spirit, that we may perfectly love thee, and worthily magnify thy holy Name; through Christ our Lord. *Amen.*' That is a lovely prayer which says so much. If we are going to pray together, we need to learn to be brief. Lengthy prayers have put a lot of people off.

When Sir Wilfred Grenfell was a medical student in London, on the way home from college one night he saw a big tent. Wandering in, he found himself in the middle of a revival meeting. There was a man on the platform praying, and he prayed on and on and on. Wilfred, who had no Christian interest, just pure curiosity, got up to go out of the door —when the chairman of the meeting stood up and said, 'Friends, let's sing a chorus while our brother finishes his prayer' — and the whole congregation burst into song. Grenfell was so taken with the commonsense of this man that he said, 'I'm staying', and he was converted, later going out to Labrador as a missionary. (I find that exciting, don't you?) We can be thankful that the chairman cut the lengthy prayer short!

The next problem is stereotyped prayers. There are those who pray the same thing all the time, who even in extemporary prayer have their own 'liturgy'. There was a man who used to pray every week in the prayer meeting, 'Lord, sweep the cobwebs from our heart.' They got so sick of it that one day a young man at the back got up and said, 'Lord, kill that spider. Amen!'

There are ways of dealing with people who get stereotyped. I think the Lord wants us to be able to laugh at ourselves sometimes. You may have heard of Professor Norman Snaith. If you know anything about Old Testament theology, you will know that he was one of the foremost scholars in Britain. He had a rather disconcerting way when he took college prayers in Leeds. He would always come into the college chapel, go up to the prayer desk at the front and say, 'Good morning, Lord.' This grated on some of the students. And it went on, and on and on — always 'Good morning, Lord.' So, finally, one day he came in and said, 'Good morning,

Lord' — and a student at the back said, 'Morning, Snaith!' He never did it again! There are ways of curing these things. But to come to something quite serious, we can easily get into a rut with our phraseology, and it kills a prayer meeting. When we come to a prayer meeting, we need to pray, 'Lord, make me fresh this morning.'

Problem number five is people who pray in public as if they were alone. This is a rather deeper problem. There are those who pray a prayer that would have been more appropriate in their bedroom. I mean by that those who are 'I, I, I', in public, and those who, in a sense, draw attention to themselves and their own spiritual pilgrimage. When we come to pray together, we should not be preoccupied with ourselves, we should seek to pray the kind of prayer that will bring others with us to the throne of grace, and that takes a little care, to avoid translating or transferring your bedroom prayer into the church prayer meeting.

Finally, there is the problem of discontinuity. By this I mean that in a prayer group the Lord gives a flow, and he has a pattern which he fits together, so that each prayer flows from the previous one and it evolves. Listening carefully to the flow of prayer, and listening to the previous person, and knowing that now it is right for me to come in with my little prayer — it just fits there. You can be in a lovely session of thanksgiving and you are just being led towards praise, then somebody who maybe got in late comes right out, 'Lord, please bless Mrs Smith, she's gone to hospital as you know' — and the whole continuity has been broken. There is a place, and the Lord will lead on to the time when it is right to pray for Mrs Smith. But when we pray together we should be very sensitive and say, 'Where is the Spirit leading us in prayer?' Listen to the prayers before you, don't just hold your prayer in your mind and think, 'Right, when someone stops I'll get mine in. Say, 'Lord, when do you want mine in?' — so that it flows, and the Lord is able to lead the prayer meeting. These are some of the practical problems.

So we have looked at the biblical basis, the added advantage, and the practical problems, now the 'concentric circles'. It is as if you drop a stone into a pond and the circles just get bigger and bigger. The first circle of prayer is two or three. And if you feel it difficult in a larger prayer meeting may I suggest that you find two other people and get together and say, 'Let's meet once a fortnight or something, and simply pray together. I'm scared of ten or twelve people, but I wouldn't mind just two of you coming, and I would learn to pray.' That is the initial cell, and frankly I would rather see a hundred cells than one big church prayer meeting, because I think that is going to encourage more prayer. Cellular growth is natural.

Billy Graham went to a town once, and the first night he had the biggest response to his appeal of any first night of any crusade he had ever conducted. He could not understand it, it was so out of the pattern. So he made careful inquiries, and discovered two elderly, unmarried, invalid ladies who could not leave their home, but who had prayed together for six years that God would visit that town — just two ladies together! And Billy was astonished at the result. So first there is the tiny cell. In fact, Peter mentions in his letter that the smallest cell can be husband and wife praying together.

The next circle is the prayer meeting, anywhere

between ten and a hundred. Now the problems become a little more acute, but the possibilities are also great. I have told you about the Shanghai church, but let me just mention that I think it is important to join the boiler to the engine, and for the people in the prayer meeting to be involved in the practical side of the church, and *vice versa*, for the people in the practical side to be involved in the prayer side, otherwise you develop two churches – the 'Marthas' and the 'Marys' – and they need each other. But there is the larger church, and there are times when the church needs to get together for prayer.

The third circle, larger still, is the public service. Here we have a larger difficulty of praying together. It is a difficulty because there are so many of us.

Let me tell you how intoning began — you may not know. Before artificial aids to voice production, when massive cathedrals were built they used to go into the cathedral and sing up a scale, and when they then hit the right note the building vibrated. They then prayed on that note, and that was the origin of intoning parts of services and it was very sensible, though it is quite unnecessary now that we have PA equipment. It is still terribly important, though, that everybody should hear, and that they should be together.

As I have already pointed out, there is a real place for prayers from books. What is using a hymn book but praying together? You need more co-ordination, and there is a place for using words together which have been prepared for us, so that we can be more united as a large group. That is why we use free prayers and prayers from books; sing hymns together, and read passages together; and it is why we sing hymns at all. It is quite silly to think that it is more spiritual to sing without books, or to pray without books, or to be totally spontaneous. The larger the crowd the more important it is almost to have words that can quickly unite a large group of people into a common prayer. The saying of the grace is an example of that. Incidentally, the sound of a grand amen is a great encouragement. Do not be afraid to say amen or hallelujah if you really are with a prayer. However large the congregation, the Lord loves the sound of a great amen. It is a word that we can all get together in, and offer to him.

Then there is a larger circle still — of the church of Jesus Christ throughout the world. Whenever any one of us joins in prayer in a service, we are not alone, we join with the whole church throughout the world. We are praying with the saints. Hallelujah! There is a complete twenty-four hour cycle of prayer going on at this moment.

Do you know the hymn *The day thou gavest, Lord, is ended*? It includes these lines,

> *As o'er each continent and island*
> *The dawn leads on another day,*
> *The voice of prayer is never silent,*
> *Nor dies the strain of praise away.*

In prayer we are one link in the chain of prayer around the world, we are praying with the saints.

Finally, there is a bigger circle still, and it includes heaven as well as earth: 'with angels and archangels, and with all the company of heaven' —words out of a book, but don't they mean something to you? They suggest that we are in a very big circle. Private prayer? There is no such thing. I remember going to see a dear old lady who lived alone, who had very few people to visit her — a lovely saint of God. She was cut off from all prayer meetings except when somebody went to see her and they prayed together. I said, 'How do you manage? Don't you find it a bit discouraging?' She said 'no', and I'll never forget her saying it. She said, 'As I lie in the bed here, when I pray, all the angels join in with me.' She held a prayer meeting every time she prayed. She never prayed privately, she was surrounded whenever she prayed in that little room! She had discovered that Christian prayer is prayer with the saints.

Now why should it please God more when we meet together? Why should prayer be more powerful with heaven when we meet together? There must be a reason for this. Though I have made a little promise to my children about not mentioning them when writing, I am going to ask their forgiveness for just mentioning one thing. I remember when they were doing their exams the three of them got together and they drew up a document for me to sign. They had a long consultation about it and decided what it was worth to their father's pride if they got pass, distinction and so on, and they carefully worked out some sums down the side. Then they agreed on this and they brought it together to me to sign, so that their labours would be rewarded financially! So I carefully read it through and I said, 'Well, there's just one thing missing and that is there's nothing down here about how much you owe me if you fail!' So they went back and had another think, and worked out how much they felt they would owe me if they failed. We carefully drew up the document and I signed it, and it was put away somewhere safe in the house from where it would be produced at the appropriate time. I am a father, so is God. The point is that a father responds much more when children have got together and agreed, when they are relating to each other in something. So if they want something really badly, let them get together in love and in good relationships, and agree together, and the very fact that they have agreed together and come with their request means it is not easy for a father to resist. Why? You love to see your children co-operating, don't you? God is a Father and he loves to see his family agree. He loves to see them in unity; he loves to see them of one heart and of one mind. He poured out his Spirit at Pentecost when they were not only in one place but when they were with one accord. He had got a family to bless, and he wants to fill his body with his Spirit; he wants to fill his family with love; he wants to give gifts to us, so he looks down from heaven and waits for his children on earth to agree, co-operating and coming as a family. I cannot explain all the New Testament teaching on praying with the saints on any other ground than such an understanding of the ways of the Father in heaven, after whom every family on earth is made. So let us come boldly to the throne of grace, and find his grace to help us.

PRAYER

Father, we thank you for togetherness in the Lord. We thank you that it is your will that we should pray together, that we should love one another, and bring our requests to you, together. Thank you for the power of united prayer. Lord, I pray now that everybody in our church will not only come to services but will meet in prayer with some others, in however small a group, so that there may be such a wave of prayer that we will see you do great things in your power. Lord, we pray for a praying church, and groups of people with vision who are agreed and walking in love, and who come as children together and say, 'Dad, will you do this because we have agreed?' We know that you love us and you want to glorify your name through us. We ask it in Jesus' name, and for his sake. *Amen.*

6

PRAYER BY MYSELF

Let us summarise what we have noticed so far about the distinctiveness of Christian prayer.

First, it is prayer to a Father. No other religion has that kind of prayer — to come to your heavenly Dad, and call him that is something no other religion has dared to teach, and which sounds to many people too intimate, too familiar.

Secondly, I have explained that prayer, for the Christian, is prayer to Jesus, and we can get his signature to the petition, and when you get his signature you get the answer, you get the prayer, you 'get the cheque cashed' — and that is something no other religion has.

Thirdly, Christians alone in the world can pray *in*

the Spirit. We are going to look at what that means. Nobody is very good at prayer. By nature we are not good at it, and God knows that perfectly well. He knows that we do not know how to pray as we ought, but the Spirit helps us in our weakness. And no other religion can offer the Spirit of God to help with this weakness, so that makes Christianity special.

Fourthly, when we pray, we pray against the devil, and I have already given you some hint of what that can mean in practical terms. You pray against the devil and he will attack you, and one of his favourite weapons is sickness. He can bind people that way. So that is a different dimension to prayer. Frankly, the devil does not bother much about other kinds of prayer because they do not do much anyway, and he goes after the live ones, not the dead ones.

We have also looked at praying with the saints, and there are few experiences as lovely as getting together with a group of people who know God. Talking together to him, and praying with the saints, is unique. You can pray with other people in other religions, but you can only pray with the saints in the Christian religion. And the saints are those who are not *trying* to get through to God, but those who have already got through and are on their way to glory.

Now we to turn to prayer *by myself*, not about 'private prayer' but about *secret* prayer. That distinction may sound like no more than a quibble, but by 'secret prayer' I mean prayer that is not seen by other people; by 'private prayer' I mean prayer that is me and God alone, and I have shown you that there is no such thing for the Christian as private prayer. If I get on my knees, the devil, principalities and powers are after me, the Father is listening to me, Jesus is involved, the Spirit is helping me, the saints are surrounding me, and I feel upheld by the little group of believers that is praying for me now. So it is not *private* prayer, but it can be *secret* and our Lord called it that. He said, *'When you pray, go into a room and shut the door, and your Father who sees in secret . . . .'* He never used the word private. Someone said that the secret of religion is religion in secret, and that is a useful little cliché.

The Bible is full of exhortations to secret prayer.

Matthew chapter 6, the Sermon on the Mount, says it. Jesus does not say, 'If you pray', he says, *'When you pray'*; he does not say, 'If you give', he says, *'When you give'*; he does not say, 'If you fast', he says, *'When you fast'*. He assumes that all three will be part of your normal life – giving, praying, fasting – and he exhorts you to go into a room, shut the door, and get alone with God that way. The Bible is packed with examples of this. If you study the life of any great person in the Bible, whether it is Abraham, Moses, Elijah, Daniel, you will find that they learned how to get alone with God. Above all, if you look at our Lord Jesus Christ you will find that, time and time again, he went up into the hills to have a chat with his Father. This is what we are looking at now.

In theory this ought to be the easiest thing for the Christian to do. After all, if you love someone, don't you want to spend as much time as you possibly can with them? When I met and fell in love with my wife I was travelling with a Christian colleague around Yorkshire, Nottinghamshire and Lincolnshire. We were evangelising wherever we could. We went down coal mines and talked to men at the coal face; we were going into the pubs; anywhere we could get hold of people, we were going together. The man I was travelling with noticed that I disappeared for long stretches of time. I never told him where I had been, and he quickly realised I was in love. When you really love someone, you do not say, 'Oh dear, I'll have to try and spend at least half an hour with them today.' If someone talked like that, would you assume that they were in love? Of course not. So, in theory, if I love Jesus I should find it the easiest thing in the world to spend a lot of time with him, yet in practice many Christians find it one of the most difficult things to do.

I want to be very practical. As far as prayer is concerned I am still in the primary department, and I am very much aware of the saints who have got very close to God and could teach me a thing or two. Having said that, I want to deal with this very practical problem: why, in theory, if I love my Jesus should it ever be difficult to spend hours with him? If it were my wife, I would have gone around the British Museum in spiked shoes for six hours just to be with her, and it would not have to be interesting at all —because love just makes you want to be with someone, and you are at ease and you are not stuck for what to talk about. Why then should one have difficulty with prayer?

How do you feel when you sing a hymn or Christian song and the words express a love for the Lord which at that moment you do not feel? Do you feel a bit guilty about singing the words? If so, I am going to try to help you, because false guilt is about the worst foundation on which to build your prayer life. You do have to be honest with yourself, and to know that the Lord wants you to pray and he wants you to receive any help you need.

In practice the difficulty varies from temperament to temperament. For example, if you are an extrovert, an outgoing person, then you will find it easier to pray with the saints than to pray by yourself. If you are an introverted or more inward-looking person, you may have found it easier to pray by yourself than to pray with the saints. Some of us have a bigger problem than others about praying secretely, as some of us have a bigger problem than others in a prayer meeting. But most of us find that we face difficulties at times.

There is a very simple and a very obvious reason why we find it difficult to say, 'I love Jesus, therefore I have no difficulty in spending hours with him and talking to him.' I remember a young people's gathering one Sunday evening. We were sitting on our lawn and we had a very honest discussion. Someone said, 'Why is it more difficult to spend hours with Jesus than it is with my boyfriend [or girlfriend]?' It was explained to the group that if I fall in love with a human being, what makes it easy to be with them is first that I am able to communicate with them through my physical senses, so there is an outward sense of their presence — I can see them, hear them, touch them, and smell them, if they use perfume or aftershave! The outward sense of their presence gives inward sensations which may be pleasurable. But when I try to pray with Jesus, the outward sense of presence is absent, and the inward one often can be, and that provides the problem.

When I was courting my wife, I had an outward sense of her presence. I could hold her, I could kiss her, I could talk to her, and I had an inward sensation while I did, which made the whole thing delightful. But when you are in a room with someone you cannot see, cannot hear, cannot touch, cannot smell, and when you are in a situation where there is no inward sensation responding to that presence, you have a problem. If you have never had that problem then you can put this book down right now. There are times when you are so aware of the presence of Jesus that he is almost too real, it is almost too much. That is probably not every time, though.

So how are we going to get over these problems? Some readers may remember how on old-fashioned coin-operated telephones there was a 'button A' which one needed to press, in order to make the coins drop and complete the connection. Well, one man said to me, 'Prayer to me is like speaking into a telephone without pressing button A.' He said, 'It is just like talking to myself. I don't seem to get through.' I heard of one schoolboy who did that to his headmaster. The headmaster had caned him and he was feeling very resentful and bitter, so he rang up the headmaster and then, without pressing button A, he told him exactly what he thought of him, and it certainly worked something out of his system! Some people suspect that prayer is a bit like that: it is good to talk it out, it is good to pray, but you are really just on a telephone with nobody hearing at the other end. But that is not prayer. Prayer is a two-way conversation. So there may be a feeling of unreality we have to get over.

On one occasion, when I was driving north from Jerusalem to Samaria, I saw the Helen Keller School, which serves the needs of children with sensory impairment (including visual impairment, hearing impairment, and the deaf/blind, as well as, in many cases, additional multiple disabilities) – and my mind went back to that amazing woman, Helen Keller. She was born blind and deaf, and so was dumb, for since she never heard words, she could not speak them, and was therefore unable to communicate with her environment and even her family, except through touch. Lacking the senses that we most use to contact others, she had a battle. A lady named Ann Sullivan took Helen and taught her; they battled, they fought, and it was a real battle. But she got through to the point where she was in communication with people, and could talk to and listen to others, exerting a very great influence. As I thought of Helen Keller it occurred to me that this is the problem we have with prayer. By nature I am blind to the Lord, I am deaf to the Lord, and therefore I am dumb and I do not know how to talk. I have to learn to communicate without the senses, for every other relationship I have had has been through my senses, and this one cannot be, so I will have to learn — but if Helen Keller could learn then I can, especially as I have a better teacher than Helen Keller had, because the Holy Spirit is a great teacher and he really wants me to get over this problem and to be aware that the person to whom I am praying is just as really in my presence as if my wife were there. That is, I think, the ultimate objective of our early struggles in prayer.

There are many things we have to learn as a duty before they become a delight, and this can be so with prayer. Do you remember doing your scales, if you learnt to play the piano? Was it a duty or a delight? If you enjoy playing the piano today it is because you learned to get over those early problems. Do you remember the time you learned to drive? The kangaroo clutch! After the first two or three lessons, maybe you despaired, you became frightened of the thing, until your teacher went on forcing you to get over those problems.

Now I trust that you have reached the stage where it is a delight and you enjoy driving. No matter what it is, think of something that you really enjoy doing and ask: was there not a time at the beginning when it was more a duty than a delight? If it is something really worth doing, then there was a time when you had to roll up your sleeves and get down to it, and go on until you got over the problem. I am not going to promise you an easy path to the presence of God, I am going to say that it need not remain a duty and it will not, but that there may be an element of duty, an element of sheer self-discipline, especially when you begin.

Earlier, to make a point, I compared the love that I have for my wife with the love I have for the Lord, or, rather, how that love translates into actions. Of course, I cannot define the love for the Lord in terms of my love for my wife, and you cannot do that either, because it is a different kind of love. The Greeks had different words for such different kinds of love. However, there are some parallels in how love should be expressed — in the areas of loyalty and duty, for example. How did our Lord express his love for me? By having a nice bubbly feeling about me? No, he expressed his love by determinedly going through with something he did not want to do, and did not feel like doing: he went to the cross. That is how he showed his love for me. If I am going to show my love for him, then I must be prepared to go through something which is going to produce the results he desires. There is an element of loyalty in divine love, and in duty; it is an element that has to be added to human love to make it worthwhile.

What are we doing in a wedding service? Are we just recognising that two people have fallen in love with each other? No, because that is not enough to see them right through; it is not firm enough, it is not strong enough. They have been going out together, they enjoy each other's company, they feel for each other, they are stimulated by each other, they share interests. That is not enough. The couple will be asked to add loyalty to the love, they will be asked to add duty to it, they will be asked to promise solemnly that they will never separate but will stay together for better, for worse, for richer for poorer, until death parts them. They need some divine love with their human love, and to see the duty as part of their love; and even if you do not always feel on Monday morning, when washing up the breakfast things, the same as you felt on the honeymoon, it is still love because it is loyalty. If you love your Lord, you will show your love for him not by having a nice bubbly feeling inside but by keeping his commandments, by doing your duty. That is the love he taught. And it is only those who learn to do their duty who learn that it is a delight. That is the first thing. There is a certain amount of self-discipline involved.

You need not shut off feelings from your prayer life — so please do not do that. Some Christians are so frightened of their feelings getting out of hand that they convince themselves that they do not have feelings, and that is sad. But let your feeling be hooked onto your faith, do not let your faith be hooked onto your feelings.

Let me tell you what I mean by that. You may feel like praying at church, away from the boss, away from work. The next morning you may feel quite different — you do not feel like talking to the Lord. But I want you to to exercise faith at that point and remind yourself that the facts of the situation are totally unchanged since Sunday night. Has God died since Sunday night? No. Has Jesus said he is not going to come back to earth since Sunday night? No. Is the kingdom not going to come now? No, it is coming, nothing has changed, so my faith can be just the same, even though I feel 'Monday morningish'. Therefore, I can pray on my faith. And as I reflect that God is still on the throne and Jesus is still coming, and the kingdom is still going to come, my feelings rise to match my faith — so do not cut feelings out, just let faith pull your feelings along and facts pull your faith along.

Now a word of caution at this point: you can regard your prayer in the same spirit as you might regard a cold bath. Do you know what I mean? If it is only duty, and it never gets beyond that, it is like a kind of cold bath every morning: set the alarm, grit your teeth, and get down. But you will not find it a delight while you are doing it.

So how do we discover that God really is there — that the Lord Jesus is actually listening to our prayer? There are two things I am going to look at.

Firstly, I think that from persisting in the duty of praying we come to the second stage, where we know he was there through hindsight. This, I would say, is stage number two. Stage number one: you are praying and wondering if he is listening, but you are doing it because you know you have to learn, and you are doing it because he has given you the strength to do it. Stage number two: you have done it without feeling his presence, but what happened afterwards proved that he was there.

My mind goes back to what occurred when the disciples first met Jesus following his resurrection, when they were aware of his presence. They could touch him, they could see him, they could hear him, and he said, *'Peace be to you'* —and it was great, they had Jesus with them. Thomas came into the room shortly afterwards. They told Thomas that Jesus had been there. Thomas did not know what he had missed. But Thomas said he did not believe it. He wanted to see for himself. He looked all around the room and did not see a soul. His Jesus had holes right through his hands and a great gash through his side — so until he could put his fingers through that hole, and until he could put his hand right through that gash, you would not catch him believing what they said. A week later, in the same room, Jesus said, *'Thomas, come and put your finger through my hands, and put your hand down by my side'* —and Thomas says, *'My God, you are here.'*

Do you get the message? Between the resurrection and the ascension, Jesus was teaching those disciples to have an awareness of his presence even without any of the senses. That is why it took six weeks between the resurrection and the ascension. And for six weeks Jesus was coming and going, until they did not know whether he was coming or going — until, finally, they knew that when he went he had not gone! This is what the Bible teaches. On the day Jesus went back to heaven, and they saw the body disappear beyond the clouds, they knew that they would not be able to touch it or hear it any more. His last words at that point were: *'Lo! I am with you always.'* From now on they would not need any of the senses to know his presence. They had been weaned, and Jesus said, *'Blessed are those who won't even have the chance to see me that you have had, but who believe in my presence.'* The ascension means that he is beyond the reach of our senses. People say, 'I could believe in him if you produced him, if he walked into church and preached one Sunday night that would be great.' But without any of my senses I know that Jesus is here now — maybe I cannot hear him, cannot see him, cannot touch him, but he is right here. The ascension means that: *'Lo! I am here with you always, even to the end of the world.'*

How do you know? Often it is about hindsight — in other words, getting an answer later. When believers talk of their prayers having been answered, they know he was present because in hindsight look what happened; he must have been listening. This means that you have more confidence to pray. It is more than a duty, it is becoming a privilege, because as Spurgeon said, 'Prayer bends the omnipotence of heaven to your desire.' In response to prayer, God changes his mind. He does not change his character; our prayer does not change who he *is*, but it does change what he *does*. There are many examples in the Bible of people who have been bold enough to argue with God. Moses did, and God changed his mind and did something different. He did not change his character, but Moses pleaded with God so effectively that God changed his mind, and the Bible says that God repents, he changes his mind (which is what the word 'repent' means). Sometimes, when you look back in hindsight, you know that God has done something that he would not have done if you had not prayed.

At some point there begins to occur such an amazing series of coincidences that statistically you know he was listening, and you are confident to pray, even though you do not feel his presence, because you know he is listening, as so many such things have happened.

* * * * *

When you pray, the reply may not be what you asked for. The encouragement that we are looking for may be received, though, as we get our reply. Frankly, it can be more satisfying to get a reply than to get a request fulfilled. There is a solemn

214

text in the Psalms which says that God gave them his desire, and he sent leanness into their souls; he gave them what they wanted, and they got thin spiritually. God replies, and it is his replies that take us into what I have called 'stage two' of prayer. Job said, *'What profit do we get if we pray to him?'* The answer is that you get a reply, and the reply encourages you to go on praying. When you are praying, you are praying to a Father and a King. If you are praying to a King, then you can bring big things to him, but if you are praying to a Father you can bring small things to him — isn't that a lovely thought? If he is a Father, then he knows how many hairs there are on my head, and he notices when a sparrow hops to the ground. A King deals with big matters, a Father deals with the little things that are big to his children, so I can come and get a reply.

'Stage three' of prayer is the stage of what I want to call *insight*. I want to go beyond knowing afterwards that he was present, and ask: can I know each time I pray that he is present while I pray? Can I feel his presence every time, or not? In the last analysis, that will be the biggest encouragement to prayer. As long as I am in stage one, doing it because I know it is right, determined to keep his commandments to show my love for him, but not sensing his presence at all, it is pretty tough going. When I get into stage two, and start getting answers, it becomes that much easier to go on praying, because I know things are happening as a result. But you still may be without the sense of his presence at the moment. There is a stage three and, praise God, when you get through to stage three you know as you talk he is in the room.

Now how does that come about? There is no technique, and yet as I read my Bible I notice that again and again people talk to God with such a vivid sense of his presence that they just chatted with him. Have you noticed that? Have you ever found yourself thinking, 'If only I could talk to God like Moses, have a conversation with him and get an immediate answer, and know that he is there'? Well, how does that happen?

I do not believe there is a technique that will help you to realise the presence of God. I have read many books on prayer and I have studied many techniques. Some say sit, some say stand, some say kneel, some say lie on the ground, some say go for a walk, some say keep your eyes open, some say shut your eyes, some say go into your bedroom, some say use a particular street on your way to work, some say get into the country away to the hills, some say this and some say that —and the techniques just leave you a little bewildered. Mind you, one lady said that since I said use your hands she has found that God has given her the prayer to pray. I said to her, 'God has given you a real gift for discernment in prayer, you are praying for just the right things when you are in a prayer group, the right things that you don't know about.'

She replied, 'Since I started to use my hands like this, he has given me the prayer to pray.' That is lovely, but I am not going to stress techniques. I think the most important thing for you in prayer is to be relaxed and related to God, and if you are more relaxed and related sitting down, then sit down; if you are more relaxed and related on your knees, then get on your knees; if you are more relaxed and related with your eyes open, then keep your eyes open; if you are more relaxed and related with your eyes shut, shut them. Experiment, vary, until you find what is right for you. There is no technique that is right for everybody, but the important thing is this: can I get through to the point where I am so relaxed and so related that I know he is there in the room with me, and that he is talking to me? The answer is that you can. It will not be with the body, because our senses are bodily; it will not even be with the mind, because the mind can so easily get in the way, with wandering thoughts and with other things.

I will tell you how I think it is done. If you are a Christian there is another part of your personality that has now come to life. You are not body and mind alone (or, as the Greeks would have expressed it, body and soul alone), you are also spirit, and it is the spirit that can be made aware of the presence of Jesus in the room. In other words, there is a depth of relationship that is far deeper than the body and the mind can have. Human relationships are generally limited to body and mind, or body and soul. As long as those two get together, you can have a lovely friendship or a lovely marriage. Sometimes with another human being you can be so deep with the person that you just know each other — you can be silent, and you know each other's thoughts, and deep down you know each other's feelings. And the relationship with God can be at a deeper level — deep calling to deep; Spirit calling to spirit.

Many of the gifts of the Spirit bypass the mind altogether. Those who trust their intellect do find it very difficult indeed to believe that there is another dimension, where the human spirit can commune with the Spirit of God, and words can go from Holy Spirit to human spirit that do not come anywhere near the brain, and do not come from the mind —where spirit just *knows*.

When Holy Spirit touches your spirit you can get rid of an intellectual barrier that so many of us have which restricts our prayers to prayer with the mind. Though there is a place for the latter. As Paul says, *'I will pray with the mind and I will pray with the spirit.'* If you have never prayed with your spirit, you have missed out on a real dimension to prayer. I will sing with the mind and I will sing with the spirit. I will have both kinds of prayer in my life, both kinds of singing. I will come to what I mean by prayer in the Spirit, but there is a deep level when the spirit knows that Jesus is there.

I would like to give you a personal testimony. As I wrote, I reached a point where I said, 'Jesus, are you in the room with me?' and my spirit just 'burst'. There was a motion that followed it quickly, but it was not emotion. My body and mind caught up with my spirit in a few minutes, but my spirit *knew* that Jesus was there, and I could 'pour out' from my spirit to him. I believe that is the point at which you can know the presence of the Lord when you pray, when his Spirit is making his presence known to your spirit. It is at that depth. I cannot explain it and I cannot describe it, but I tell you this: some saints take years to get through to the point where they know that Jesus is there as they talk; they have occasional experiences of it which are not regular. Or, as they grow in grace through many years, they get to the point where, more or less every time in prayer, they know Jesus is with them. But I have great news for you, there is a little bit of a short cut available to this, and it is to be *drenched* in the Holy Spirit. I do not care what term you use – baptised in Holy Spirit, filled with Holy Spirit, anointed with Holy Spirit, have the Holy

Spirit poured on you, fall upon you – but I tell you this, when your spirit is drenched with his Spirit you will know his presence very deep down. You will not argue about it, your mind will not get in the way. In fact, he will just put your mind out of the way because it is a bit of an intrusion.

When he baptises in Holy Spirit, it seems as if he releases in a person's prayer life this immediate sense of the presence of God so that their spirit can commune with God's Spirit, with the Lord, with the Father; and his Spirit witnesses with your spirit that you are a child of God, so you can shout, 'Daddy, Abba, Father.' It is the Spirit telling me, at the level of my spirit. My bodily senses say he is not in the room, my mind wanders and says, 'Well, maybe my mind can check up later on the answers and see whether he really has been listening', but when the Spirit bears witness with my spirit, body and mind get out of the way and my spirit is aware of the presence of Jesus. That is why, if you are having problems with the sense of his presence in your prayer, may I suggest you start praying that he will fill you with his Spirit, that he will drench you in his Spirit. And I tell you, you will be more aware of his presence than you ever were before that prayer is answered, and it is a prayer he loves to answer.

It is glorious! This is open to any Christian, whatever condition their body is in, and whatever condition their mind is in. I went to see a member of the church who was dying. For three to four days the family had been unable to get any response whatsoever from that person lying there in a deep coma — no physical response, no mental response. I called an hour or two before that church member died, and one of the family said, 'It's no use, do you want to go in?' I said yes and went in. I sat by the bed and put my mouth close to that near-corpse's ear, and said, 'I am going to pray, and I want you to join with me', and I began, 'Our Father, who art in heaven' —and I got no further, and the lips said, 'Hallowed be thy Name. Thy kingdom come. Thy will be done.' It was not really the body that was doing that, and it was not the mind, it was the spirit that was still very much alive. And I am talking about this third depth in prayer, the point at which God wants to commune with you and give you an awareness of his presence.

At one time I was chaplain to a hospital for mental patients, and I would go and take a service once a week. I often wondered whether I was wasting my time, because it was a ward for those who, medically speaking, would never get out of there and would never recover. All sorts of strange things happened. When I announced a hymn, a man used to stand up and salute, all the time we sang; the music must have touched some deep, subconscious memory of military bands. I was talking to the man in charge of that section, and I said, 'You know, sometimes I wonder if anything gets through.' He said, 'Mr Pawson, please don't stop coming. The only time in the week they behave differently is during this service. The only rational words some of them utter are the words of the hymns.' Spirit.

You see, there is a level of enjoying the presence of God which is not at the level of bodily senses. It is not even at the level of mental deduction. ('He must have been there because we prayed and he answered'). It is *spiritual* awareness, which is not limited by physical or mental condition. Hallelujah! So you can know his presence. His Spirit can bear witness with your spirit that you are a child of God, that he is your Daddy, that the Lord Jesus is listening and is ready to sign your petition; that the devil is defeated; that the saints are with you; and that even if you do not know how to pray as you ought, the Spirit can fill your mouth with a language you never learned, and set you free to pray.

PRAYER

Father, thank you that when I became one of your children you brought my spirit to life. Before then, I was spiritually dead. I spoke to you, but I was not sure if you were listening; I did not know whether I really had any reply. Lord, thank you that you did not want it to stay that way. Thank you that you have given us a new dimension of communing with yourself.

Lord, drench me with your Spirit, fill me with your Spirit —that, even if my body and mind cannot grasp your presence, my spirit may be so full of you that I have no doubt whatever that I am talking to you, and that you are talking to me. Lord, if I desire to have my bodily senses satisfied, forgive me. Thank you that one day I will see Jesus with my own eyes and hear him with my ears, but Lord, until I do, give me faith so that I do not need the senses. And, Lord, if my mind cannot understand, and if my mind is arguing, and my thoughts are wandering away from you, keep my spirit close to you, and teach me how to commune as friend with Friend, spirit with Spirit, deep to deep.

Lord, thank you for the sense of your presence at this moment. Thank you that you are really here. Lord, continue to speak to me, and help me to know you, and to love you, and to talk with you, and to listen. I ask it for your name's sake. *Amen.*

7

PRAYER FOR OTHERS

There is a sin that most of us have committed, probably regularly, which we rarely count as a sin. We regard it as an oversight, or a lapse of the memory, and here it is: *'As for me, far be it from me that I should sin against the Lord by ceasing to pray for you'* (1 Samuel 12:23). When did you last realise that was a sin, and ask forgiveness for it? It is an astonishing thing that we have overlooked that little verse. Intercession on behalf of others is regarded in Scripture as a responsibility, though it is also a privilege. As we shall see, intercession is one of the hardest aspects of prayer to learn. It is much easier to pray for yourself and your own needs than for the needs of other people. It is instinctive to pray for yourself; it is not so natural to pray for other people. Having said that, it is a delight to know when your prayer has been mightily effective for someone else. There are few joys to compare with hearing that what you have prayed for someone has been gloriously answered.

Long before I became a Christian, I came across the power of intercessory prayer. I remember vividly the Christmas morning when I woke up feeling somewhat poorly. My father went out preaching that day. While he was away I was taken terribly ill. I knew I was very ill indeed. He hurried back from the service, which he had cut short because the Lord told him in his heart that there was a serious need at home, and that it was me. Within half an hour I was in hospital with suspected meningitis. I think the family suffered more than I did. Certainly their Christmas dinner was spoilt completely. Three days later I walked out of that hospital totally well. On the Monday morning my parents brought in for me a long sheet of paper with 120 names on it of people who said, 'We believe that God has a future for David and we are going to pray together' —and here I am! But I was not a

Christian then, and though I was intrigued by how many names were on the paper, I did not then fully appreciate what those people had been doing.

By the time I became a Christian, in September 1947, I had already become aware of the power of intercessory prayer. It was a Friday night when I became a Christian. I had been staying for a week with about a hundred young people, most of whom were Christians, and it is rather disconcerting to blunder into a room and find a circle of people praying for you by name. Before you are a Christian you do not really appreciate that. Once you become a Christian you appreciate it enormously — that people loved you enough to pray for you by name. But you resent it at the time. Who do they think they are, praying for me? I suppose they think they are better than I am . . . . I had all the usual reactions. But at least I know that intercessory prayer played a vital role in my conversion on the Friday evening of that week. Ever since, I have learned how much is due to this. And I tell you, I am more aware than anyone of how much of my ministry is due to the intercession of others rather than my activities, and I could not face my ministry again and again if I did not know of those who – secretly, before the Lord – seek to uphold me by name. I could not continue to preach and teach without that.

The mechanics of intercession are a mystery to me. There are those who have tried to explain it in psychological terms: who, for example, see prayer for yourself as a refined form of auto-suggestion. I remember hearing a lecturer in psychology saying that prayer for others could be explained in terms of telepathy and the transference of thought from one person's mind to another. I am afraid I am totally unconvinced. That is an attempt to give a natural explanation of the power of intercessory prayer, but the things that happen when you pray for others cannot be explained except in terms of the supernatural.

I think of two lady missionaries in China before the communists took over. They had to go into town to pick up a large sum of money from the bank to bring back to the hospital in the hills, where they worked as missionaries, to pay the hospital staff. For various reasons they were delayed, and they only got half way home when night fell, so they had to spend the night out on the hills in what was then bandit infested territory. So they lay down and committed themselves to the Lord. In the morning they woke up, returned to the hospital and paid the staff. They had slept with this bag of money between them — a considerable sum. Some weeks later, a well-known local bandit leader, who had been shot, was brought into their hospital. They saved his life and he said to the two missionary ladies, 'I saw you a few weeks back. You were sleeping out with a bag of money, weren't you?'

'Yes.'

'We wanted that money and we didn't come and take it.'

And the missionary ladies said, 'Why not?'

'Well,' he said, 'there were the soldiers.'

'What soldiers?'

'The soldiers with you. Twenty-seven of them, we counted them.'

The two ladies came back home on furlough some months later to their little church in London, and they told this story. The church secretary, who was a meticulous man and kept the records of all the meetings and how many attended, asked,

'What date was that?' And they told him.

He looked it up in the diary and said, 'On that day our church prayer meeting had a special burden for you, and there were twenty-seven of us at the church prayer meeting, and we prayed for protection.'

Now you may try to give me a natural explanation of that, but the truth is that more things are wrought by prayer than this world dreams of.

God has so arranged it that somebody is needed who puts a hand out to him and a hand out to someone's need, and then power flows between heaven and earth. Sometimes that connection uses your hands. Many have said that when they have laid hands on someone in prayer they have felt the tingling of God's power through their arms as the link was completed. Intercessory prayer is costly, but in response to it, God sends power that flows into the person who needs help.

I believe that angels are often present as well. Read the book of Daniel. Angels are flying around; they can leave the fastest plane standing! In Daniel chapter 9, an angel goes from highest heaven to Daniel's bedroom before the end of a prayer which at most took two minutes — that is speed! God has his messengers.

As we think about praying for others, we will consider four areas. First: why we pray for others — getting our motives sorted out. Second: who we should pray for. One of the problems is that your list can easily get too big, and I want to give you some guidance as to how to keep it within compass. Third: what we should pray for when we pray for someone; and fourth, how we should pray when we pray for others.

First, why do we pray for people? The human heart is desperately wicked, says the Bible, and deceitful above all things. The problem is our motives get so mixed up that we do not really know why we are praying for a certain person. The biggest problem in praying for others is to keep self out of it, and to see to it that self-interest is not colouring the prayer for other people. I am afraid that if we are not careful we tend to pray for those people who are involved in our self-interest in some way. Why should we pray for our nation more than other nations? We have to be careful that we are not praying for our own nation more than other nations because our way of life is threatened if our country goes down. Self-interest can limit your intercession to *my* family, *my* church, *my* nation — may these prosper so that I may be happy, so that my little world may be all that I want it to be. Self-righteousness also gets in, in such peculiar ways, when we pray for others. Did you notice I said that I am referring to prayer *for* others? I want to put in a little warning about prayer *at* others. Do you know what I mean by that? It is so easy to preach in your prayers. Do you remember the Pharisee at the front of the temple? 'I' was very large in his prayer. It came five times. *I thank thee that I am not as other men are; I fast twice in the week; I give tithes of all that I possess.* Then he looked over his shoulder at the man in the back pew and he said, '*I thank thee that I am not as other men are, even as this publican.*' Now another version of that kind of prayer is, 'Lord, make all the church members as keen as I am.' Have you heard that kind of prayer? 'Lord, just quicken them all so that they are all as keen to come to the prayer meeting as I have been to come to it this morning.' Now is that any different from the self-righteousness of the

Pharisee? 'I thank you that I am not as other men are, make them all like me and we'll have a great church.' No, self-interest, self-righteousness, just plain self, can all come in.

Let me give you another very poignant example. You may be married to an unbeliever. It is an unequal yoke — it chafes, it rubs. So you get on your knees and you say, 'Lord, make my husband a Christian'; 'Lord, make my wife a Christian.' Why are you praying that? So that you may share? So that you may be happy? So that you can have a Christian home? May I suggest that if you are married to a non-Christian the best thing you can do is to pray for yourself first. Thank the Lord for them, and pray for yourself. Thank the Lord for every good quality they have, and pray that you may be a better wife or husband, and see what happens next. But we could be simply asking that our partner may be converted, to be relieved of chafing ourselves in praying.

I once heard a preacher say, 'Pray for a man for six months and his number's up.' I do not believe that. I do not believe that prayer for others manipulates them. I do not think that is the force of prayer. You cannot make another person a Christian, even by prayer. God respects the freedom of an individual. I believe that prayer for somebody else does not force the situation but it does reinforce what God is doing in it. It is not a way you can manipulate people and make them what you want them to be, it is a form of reinforcing, so that every response they make to God's power will be reinforced by your prayer for them. In this way you are not manipulating them, you are loving them, you are helping them. Remember that there were people whom Jesus invited, but he had to let them go because they did not want to accept, when it came to the push.

Therefore, whenever we pray for someone else, we should ask why we are doing so. Am I praying in any way out of self-interest? Am I, for example, praying that my son or my daughter will be something because I failed to be that, and I am projecting my ambitions into them? There have been parents who longed to be on the mission field, or who longed to go into the ministry, who have prayed every day that their son or daughter might be a missionary. Are they sure that they are not projecting their own frustrated ambitions? There are only two motives adequate for prayer for other people, and they are these: the glory of God, and the good of the person you are praying for.

You find Paul saying, *I could wish myself accursed for my brethren's sake* —which meant that he was really praying with no self-interest at all. So we need to pray for people in a selfless way. Indeed, Jesus told us to pray and to help people who could not return anything to us, so may I suggest you go through your prayer list and say, how many of these people are people from whom I could not possibly get any benefit whatsoever, but to whom I can simply give in prayer. Jesus taught that you should do that with your home. You could invite for Sunday lunch not only those who will ask you back in three months to their home, but those who have no home to ask you back to. In the same way, pray for those from whom you will never receive anything in return, and you can be sure that your intercession is for the glory of God and for the good of men.

Now that is the first point: *why* we pray; getting our motives right. Of course, none of this means that we should not pray for our own families, churches and country as well.

The second point I want to make concerns who we pray for. There are two groups of people there is no point in praying for. First, there is no use whatever in praying for those who have died. Though we can remember them and think of them lovingly, you may leave them in God's hands. There is no use in praying for the departed. It has been a practice of pagan religion, and it crept into the Christian religion, and some Christians still feel that they can do this. But I give it to you on scriptural grounds that the decisive period in a person's existence is between the cradle and the grave; we shall be judged for the things done in the body, and the moment we die there is a great gulf fixed. The Bible is absolutely plain: prayers of the dead for us, and our prayers for the dead, are ruled out by the holy word of God, so that is a group not to pray for.

There is another small group we are told in the New Testament there is no point in praying for, and that is a group of 'Christians' who have so committed apostasy, who have so turned their back on Jesus and denied him, that they have committed what is called in 1 John 5:13 the sin unto death, and John the beloved apostle, who had so much love in his heart, says, *I do not tell you to pray for those.* There comes a point, alas, where Christians have got too far from Christ to be prayed for. Having said that, pray for everybody else.

There are, however, some special groups that the Scripture tells us to pray for, and I want to ask you to make sure that they are on your prayer list. First, your enemies. The best way to get rid of an enemy is to turn him into a friend, and the best way to turn him into a friend is to pray for him. Therefore, regularly on your prayer list should be those who do not like you, or whom you do not like, or both — it is often mutual. Do you pray for those who despitefully use you? Jesus taught it, the apostles practised it. As Jesus died he looked at the soldiers gambling at his feet, and he said, *'Father, forgive them'* and he prayed for them; and when Stephen was being stoned to death, and the rocks were cracking into his skull and splitting his skin and the blood was flowing, he said, *'Father, forgive them.'* Pray for your enemies.

I know of a young man who went into the forces. He went into the barrack room, and the first night he knelt down by his bed to say his prayers, and an army sergeant on the other side of the room picked up one of his boots and he threw it very hard at this man. It split his ear open and it really hurt, but the man went on praying. So he picked up the second boot and he threw it and he was a good shot and it cut him again, and the man went on praying for the sergeant. In the morning, when the sergeant woke up, those boots were back by his bunk polished for the day, and the sergeant said, 'I have got to find out what makes a man do that.' He became a Christian. Are you sure you are praying for your enemies? Maybe that very difficult person at work, maybe a parent whom you feel does not understand you, or a child you feel is rebellious; are you praying for your enemies?

The second group the Scripture exhorts us to keep on our list are workers for the Lord. You need to pray that there shall be workers for the Lord, and pray that the Lord may lay a name on your heart so that you can go to that person in the church and say: 'The Lord has just seemed to say to me, have you considered going overseas?' or, 'Have you considered going into the ministry?' or, 'Have you considered being an evangelist?' Would it not be lovely if that happened? That is how I got into a pulpit. A converted bookmaker asked me to go to have tea with him, and he took me to a little place called Spennymoor in County Durham, which was not a very salubrious place. He took me there for a Sunday evening service which I understood he was taking. On the way there I said, 'What are you preaching about?' He replied, 'I'm not, you are!' That was my introduction. He had been praying for workers for the Lord, and the Lord had laid his hand on me. So the converted bookie gets hold of the son of a professor and says, 'You're preaching.' When workers are in the service of the Lord they need prayer. They are exposed, they are in the front line, they need prayer, and the Bible tells you to pray for them — not for their safety or for their comfort, but for their boldness, and that the Lord will open a door to his work. Have you ever noticed how often Paul says 'pray for us', 'pray for me'? And when he is in prison, he does not say pray for my freedom or my safety, he says, 'pray that I may be bold' —pray that the word of God may not be bound, pray the doors will open to it. Are you backing workers for the Lord with prayer?

Thirdly, there is another group we are told to include in our prayer list regularly: politicians. They get plenty of ridicule, sarcasm and criticism. They need plenty of prayer. Put your Member of Parliament on your list. We are told to lift up holy hands for those who are set in places of authority, because the gospel needs certain political conditions for it to be preached freely, and we are to pray that we may have a peaceable society in which the gospel is able to be freely proclaimed. Do you pray for the politicians?

A fourth group that merits special prayer is the physically sick. Prayer is a mighty weapon in the sickroom or a hospital ward.

I have given you a number of groups, but here is a word of caution: you can get into a real bog if you have a list that is too long. I do not think it is possible, unless you have been given a special ministry of intercession, to pray for too many people at once. In fact, I may be so bold as to say that four or five in one go would be enough. Better to come back fresh later and pray again, rather than simply to present God with the membership roll, or your own 'shopping list', because when you are really praying for someone it takes it out of you, it is hard work. You may feel drained after a prayer meeting which has really got under people's burdens.

Who are we to pray for? The best thing is to let the Lord decide who you should pray for, and if you think you should pray for someone then take that name to the Lord and say, 'Lord, tell me, should I put this person on my list or not?' Beware of saying glibly, 'I'll pray for you.' Bear in mind that God will hold you to that and say, 'You have sinned against the Lord by ceasing to pray.' I think it is better to be quite honest if somebody says, 'Will you pray for me?' and you do not have any clear testimony at that moment that you should. Say, 'I will ask the Lord, and if he brings you to my mind as I pray, I will pray for you' —and then you are not making any hollow promises. It is too easy for Christians to say, 'I'll pray.' So let the Lord write the list, and then he will write a list that you can cope with. If you are praying for a situation, my advice would be not to pray for everybody in it, but to ask the Lord who the key person is in that situation, and concentrate the prayer on them. Remember the Lord so loved the world that he gave his only Son, but when Jesus prayed he said, *'I pray not for the world but for these* [eleven] *you have given me out of the world.'* They were the key people in the situation. I do not know what the population of the world was then – it was a good deal smaller than it is today – but you cannot pray for the whole world, there are over six billion in it! So you can say, 'Lord, in this situation who are the key people? Who is the most important person in that situation? Who is the person who is going to unlock the situation for others? Then I will concentrate my prayer there.' If you cannot pray for the whole cabinet, pray for the Prime Minister. If you cannot pray for the whole church, pray for the pastor. Concentrate your prayer on the key people in the situation. Jesus did.

Thirdly, let us consider what we pray for. What people want and what they need are two entirely different things, and it is difficult enough to know in yourself the difference between what you want and what you need. It is even more difficult to know what another person's need is. You know they are in need; you pray sometimes for the symptoms instead of the cause. Is a person overtired? Then you could pray, 'Lord, give them refreshment and make them less tired', or you could say, 'Lord, reveal to me why they are tired, and then I will pray for the cause to be removed.' Do you see the difference? You may find yourself praying for a different thing if you ask that way. You may hear of someone who is seriously ill and your instinct is to pray immediately for their desire to get better, and say, 'Lord, heal that person', and if you just stop and think, you might find yourself praying, 'Lord, take that person quickly.' Your immediate instinct in response to a drought in Britain is to say, 'Lord, send us rain', but if you are an Elijah you might be led to say, 'Lord, keep this drought on Britain for three years to bring us to our senses, and help us to remember that rain is a gift of yours.' Do you see the difference?

So what we pray for is important, as well as who we pray for. The principle is very simple: when you are praying for someone else you are to seek their highest good, not just a good thing for them but their highest good, and in order to achieve their highest good you may find yourself praying for something that will cause them pain or suffering. I have prayed from the pulpit that if someone in the congregation does not belong to Jesus Christ, God will give them no rest until they do. That is a funny prayer, that God will give people no rest, but I am praying for their highest good. If I just said, 'Lord, give them health and wealth and happiness', the tragedy is that their highest good might be lost and they might never feel the need of the Saviour. So, if I am going to pray for a person's highest good – the very best thing for them – I may pray rather differently; I may do what the prodigal's father did, and let the son go. I may even – and here is the most terrible prayer that a church can pray, but they can do it for someone's highest good – pray that Satan may have a Christian's body that his spirit may be saved; it is called delivering someone to Satan. And Satan may get their body and fill it with disease and even kill it, but it will bring their spirit back to God. That really is praying for the highest good for people — it is a difficult prayer.

How do we know what to pray? Well, the Holy

Spirit wants to help us, and this is where a gift of knowledge and a gift of discernment comes in. As you are really seeking to pray for someone, you suddenly see that what you thought they needed was not their highest good, so you now pray for the very best for them. That is why a good father punishes his child. Why? Because he is seeking their highest good — not their immediate comfort, but the very best. Sometimes you have to use your imagination here and really put yourself in that person's situation and ask: if I were there, what would be for my very best good?

Now I come to the fourth and last thing: how we pray for others. How can we make our intercession effective? Now here again I want to issue a word of caution. Do not think quantitatively about prayer but think qualitatively. To think quantitatively is to say: 'The longer I pray for this person, the more effective it will be', but Jesus said, *'You will not be heard for your much praying or for your many words.'* It is not true that the longer you pray for someone the more effective your intercession is. But if you think qualitatively you will know that it is the deeper you pray for someone the more effective your intercession is. One person can be deeper in two minutes than another person who prays for ten minutes, for that other person in need. Or, likewise, to think quantitatively is to think: 'Now, the more people I can get to pray this prayer the better. If only I could get a hundred or two hundred, or if we could enlist ten thousand prayer partners for this crusade, somehow God listens to ten thousand more than one or two.' But the very most Jesus promised would get more attention was two or three! He never said that if you can get a hundred or two hundred he would listen even more. Because we are thinking quantitatively, we are thinking that the more names there are to a petition the more God will listen, but I have told you that God looks through the petition for one name only, and if that name is on the petition he grants it — and it is the name of Jesus. So we must not think quantitatively that if we could get a whole lot of names on this petition to God that he would listen.

Having said that, the more people that you can get to pray deeply the better. And because I think qualitatively and not quantitatively, I would rather have ten people praying for me at depth than a hundred prayer partners who were just mentioning me.

So what do I mean by deep prayer? I mean prayer that costs the person something. The effectiveness of your prayer for someone else is in direct ratio to the cost to yourself. I believe that is why, when Jesus came down and found his disciples in the valley after he had been on the mountain, and he found them unable to help a child in need, he said, *'Don't you realise that this kind of situation can only be dealt with by prayer and fasting?'* In other words, you missed the cost out of it; it did not cost you anything to pray for this boy. And that is the place of fasting in prayer: because it is costing you something — it is costing you your meal. The only merit in spending a long time praying for someone is that it is costing you time, and time is precious these days.

What did it cost you to pray? The deepest cost is this: when a woman touched the hem of Jesus' garment and was healed, goodness went out of him, and if you have really prayed for someone, some of your resources have left you and travelled to the other person; power has gone from God, but goodness has gone from you, and they have met in the person of need. If you have really prayed for someone you should be drained, and you will need then to pray for yourself, that God will replenish the supplies that have been exhausted. So what does it cost? How do you pray?

Now there are two sorts of intercessory prayer for others: in people's absence, and in people's presence. I want to mention the effectiveness of prayer with physical contact. Of course, be sensible: young men, do not go rushing off to lay hands on young ladies, we have to be practical. But physical touch can be a tremendous reinforcement of prayer. If you are praying for someone who is weak or sick, just to hold their hand is prayer, and as you pray for them the physical contact is used by God. He made the physical as well as the spiritual, and laying on of hands is effective. It is not a symbol, it is a reality; power is flowing through your hands, and that is why the laying on of hands is a particularly impressive and expressive form of prayer. It is used in the Scripture for praying for the sick; it is used in the Scripture for praying that a person may be filled with Holy Spirit; it is used in the Scripture for praying for a worker for the Lord who is facing a new task, that they may be equipped for it. So if you are in someone's presence, and it is appropriate, use your hands and lay them on, even just a hand around the shoulder or an arm around the shoulder, and God uses that physical channel to release power. These are ways to reinforce prayer and make it more powerful.

One of the elders in my church was engaged in a lovely ministry during the day. As a tutor, he answered questions sent in from many countries of the world to very simple Bible studies, through a Christian magazine. It went out and invited young Christians or enquirers from other countries to share in a correspondence course. He showed me one paper from an African boy of thirteen years of age. (It was delightful, there was such unconscious humour in it. It said, 'Please send me a Bible, but since people take Bibles out of parcels, write on the back "whoever takes this Bible will be killed"'!) This thirteen year-old boy, in utter simplicity, was wanting to get hold of the word of God. But I noticed one question that shows how important phrasing the question is, and this phrasing was clearly a colloquialism which he did not understand. The question was: 'Why does God not listen to many prayers?' The answer this boy had given was, 'Because he would get tired'! God does not get tired listening, but if you are really praying for someone else you will get tired if it is real prayer, but God can replenish the resources of those who wait on him — even youths faint and become weary, but those who wait on him shall rise up with wings like eagles.

Here is a final comment on prayer for others. When you ask for somebody else, you must be prepared for God to say, 'You answer that prayer as well as asking it.' Time and again, when you are praying for someone else, the Lord says, 'You answer that prayer; you write a letter; you pay a visit; you go and do a service' — and he tells you to do something sometimes of which you have to say, 'But Lord, I couldn't do that, I haven't the resources.'

'You go and lay hands on that person and pray for their health.'

'But I couldn't do that, Lord!'

The Lord may say, 'Sow your own prayer, get involved with me, and I will give you the power to answer the prayer.' So whenever we pray for someone else we must finish with: 'Lord, here am I. If you care to use an angel, fine, but if you want to use me, here am I, and I will deliver the goods. I am at your service.' I am on his Majesty's service.

PRAYER

Lord, I have sinned in this particular way, and have all too lightly said to someone, 'I'll pray for you', and three weeks later have forgotten all about them. Lord, save me from such shallow intercession. Lord, give me a list that I can cope with. Tell me who I should not be praying for, that you want somebody else to intercede for. Help me to know, Lord, and then help me to pray in such a way that goodness goes out from me, as well as power from you. Lord, your resources are limitless, mine are limited, but what there is I offer to you, in the knowledge that you will replace them when they are used. Thank you, then, that I can pray for other people, and thank you that time and again I may see the results of that prayer, and I want to give you the glory, in Jesus' name. *Amen.*

8

PRAYER WITHOUT HINDRANCE

From the last four chapters of the book of Job, we recall that for many months Job was not getting through to God. He believed he was in the right, and that therefore God was in the wrong to let him suffer as he did. And to the end of his life, Job never knew why God let him suffer. We know, because God has put the explanation at the beginning of the book, but Job never knew.

Then the Lord answered Job from the whirlwind. 'Why are you using your ignorance to deny my providence? Now get ready to fight, for I am going to demand some answers from you, and you must reply.'

There had been Job for months, demanding

answers from God and saying, 'You must reply' and God says:

'I am going to speak, I am going to answer, but now let me ask you for some answers, and you reply. Where were you when I laid the foundations of the earth? Tell me if you know so much. Do you know how its dimensions were determined and who did the surveying? What supports its foundations and who laid its cornerstone as the morning stars sang together and all the angels shouted for joy? Who decreed the boundaries of the seas when they gushed from the depths? Who clothed them with clouds and thick darkness and barred them by limiting their shores and said thus far and no farther shall you come, and here shall your proud waves stop? Have you ever once commanded the morning to appear and caused the dawn to rise in the east? Have you ever told the daylight to spread to the ends of the earth to end the night's wickedness? Have you ever robed the dawn in red and disturbed the haunts of wicked men and stopped the arm raised to strike? Have you explored the springs from which the seas come, or walked in the sources of their depths? Has the location of the gates of death been revealed to

you? Do you realise the extent of the earth? Tell me about it if you know. Where does the light come from and how do you get there? Or tell me about the darkness — where does it come from, can you find its boundaries or go to its source? But of course you know all this for you were born before it was created, you are so very experienced.'

The Lord continued, 'Do you still want to argue with the Almighty, or will you yield? Do you, God's critic, have the answers?'

Then Job replied to God, 'I am nothing. How could I ever find the answers? I lay my hand upon my mouth in silence, I have said too much already.'

Then the Lord spoke to Job again from the whirlwind. 'Stand up like a man and brace yourself for battle. Let me ask you a question and give me the answer. Are you going to discredit my justice and condemn me so that you can say you are right? Are you as strong as God? Can you shout as loudly as he? All right then, put on your robes of state, your majesty and splendour, give vent to your anger, let it overflow against the proud, humiliate the haughty with a glance, tread down the wicked where they stand, knock them into dust, stone-faced in death. If you can do that, then I'll agree that your own strength can save you . . . .'

Job replied to God (in chapter 42): *'I know that you can do anything and that no-one can stop you. You ask who it is who has foolishly denied your providence — it is I. I was talking about things I knew nothing about and did not understand, things far too wonderful for me. You said "Listen and I will speak, let me put the questions to you, see if you can answer them," but now I say I had heard about you before, but now I have seen you, and I loathe myself and repent in dust and ashes.'*

So the Lord blessed Job.

When you are not getting answers from God, he might just turn around and say: I am not getting answers from you, so just stop arguing and then I can bless you.

I had a real problem with the title of this last section. At first I thought I would call it 'Prayer Without Problems'—that did not seem right. Then I thought about 'Prayer Without Difficulty'. Neither of those titles was right because I knew in my heart that I could not promise you on earth prayer without problems or prayer without difficulties. The Christian life is not an easy life, and Jesus never promised that it would be. And since prayer is at the heart of it, it is sometimes going to be hard. It is going to have problems, it is going to be difficult, for many of the reasons I have already stated. Nothing worthwhile in life is easy. How do you get to the top in sport? Is it easy? And when you have arrived at the top, is it easy to stay there? Look, it is tough. You have to work really hard to get to the top, and then when you get there you cannot say, 'Fine, I've reached it, it's easy.' Sportsmen and sportswomen have to keep at it. I think of Dr Alan Redpath when he used to play rugby in the North East. He was a folk hero of my home town. Every morning he used to go into the back yard, put his shoulder against a brick wall, and push for half an hour. That is how you get into the scrum with shoulders the size he had, and he had to do it when he got to the top as well. So I could not offer you a title 'prayer without problems' or 'prayer without difficulties' because I believe that on earth it is going to be tough — not only to get to the top but to stay there. In heaven it will be easy, for you will see the Lord as he is.

So I had to think of a different title and it is 'Prayer Without Hindrance' because many of the difficulties that we have are of our own making, and the tragedy is that prayer is more difficult for most of us than it need be. It is sometimes going to be difficult anyway, but there is no sense in adding to those difficulties. Or putting it another way round, you can reduce the difficulties.

Most books on prayer that I have looked at have a chapter on 'the problems of prayer', and it can get you rather depressed! It is like the man who sat down and read a chapter or two of 'The Family Doctor' medical book —and then just waited to die! Have you ever done that — looked up all the symptoms and thought, 'I have got this, and that, and that', and you just give up? So I am not going to go through the problems of prayer, I am only going to write about one hindrance to prayer. It has five parts to it, but to me there is only one basic problem in prayer. All the others relate to it in one way or another, so I am only going to write about one, and it is the problem of unanswered prayer.

Before we go any further, I think I have used the wrong words for that, because many people – particularly unbelievers – think of unanswered prayer as asking for something and not getting what you ask for, and that is not what I mean by the problem of unanswered prayer. The problem for most Christians of unanswered prayer is not that they do not get what they ask, but that they do not get any reply. That is the problem. There are many answers to my prayer. I may be quite convinced that I want something, and I ask for it, and the answer that God gives me may be: 'No, you can't have it, it is not good for you.' Or his answer may be, 'Wait, the time is not ready to give you that.' But that is not a problem, because there has been an answer. The problem is when the heavens seem like brass, and you feel God is not listening and you are not getting through, and it is no fun having a one-way conversation. That, I believe, is why we give up; that, I believe, is the most discouraging thing in prayer.

You do not mind God saying no if he says it. Think of Paul. Three times he said: Lord, will you deal with my physical handicap; I just cannot cope with it; I could serve you much better if I were free. I could get around much better; take away this thorn in the flesh —and three times he prayed it. Finally, God said: I can bring more glory to my name through your weakness, and giving you the grace in the weakness. Paul was happy — it was not an unanswered prayer, it was an answered prayer. It was not the answer he had hoped for, but it was an answered prayer.

Many of the greatest saints have known this problem of unanswered prayer. They have referred to it in various terms. Sometimes they have called it 'a dry experience', as it seems like going through the desert. It seems barren and fruitless. Other people have talked about it in terms of darkness rather than dryness, and there is a phrase used by many of the saints in their writings – I think St Teresa used it first – the 'dark night of the soul'. Darkness, dryness. Others have talked about it in terms of deadness — when it seems as if the life has gone out of your prayer. Others have spoken about it in terms of dullness; they have been honest and said they are bored with praying. But all of these complaints are due to the fact that they are not getting replies. It is one-way, so it is not a conversation at all. How long can you keep up a conversation if the other person will not open their mouth? Even with a human being it is difficult, and therefore with God it is very discouraging if there is no reply.

Now Job went through this experience for many months, and he tried and tried to get through. I was looking for one thing, and I found it on page after page: answer me, incline your ear, hear my prayer, hear my cry.

Again and again it appears in the Psalms: Why do you hide your face from me? Why aren't you listening to me? I am crying; I am praying. Why don't you hear? Even David, the master of psalms and prayers and praise, had this experience. I believe that all other problems relate to this. That is when wandering thoughts take over, when you feel you are not being listened to. It is when deadness takes over; when discouragement sets in; when you stop praying; when you feel it is not doing anything and not getting through, and not getting above your bedroom ceiling. I am trying to be utterly practical. I am writing in the primary department. I realise that I have no authority to speak beyond this, but nevertheless I want to help ordinary folk like myself to get over this. If I can help you in this one it is going to be well worthwhile.

There are five major causes of this problem and it could be any one of the five. Take this as a kind of self-diagnosis kit. If your car grinds to a halt and you do not belong to the AA, you go through certain things. You think: petrol, ignition . . . and you go through about five simple things and you soon get to it. I want to give you five very simple things to look at. Three are breakdowns in communication on the 'you' side, on the earthly side; two of them are a breakdown in communication on the heavenly side. Maybe you have dialled a phone number, and you have got through, but you have to say to the person on the other end, 'I'm sorry, I just can't hear you, can you hear me?' —and they say, 'Yes, I can hear you perfectly.' You say, 'Well, will you speak up, or I'll ring you back.' Then you get both sides working properly. So we are going to ask: on which side has the break in communication occurred? Is it on earth? In which case it is one of three things. Or is it in heaven? In which case it is one of two things.

Here are the three things on earth that could break down your communication:

1. That you are not right with God.
2. That you are not right with other people.
3. That you are not right with yourself.

These are the three basic causes of breakdown on the earthly end. You may still say the words, you may still pray, but communication has broken down at your end.

First: when you are not right with God. There are two ways in which that can happen. You may be sinning against him in attitude or you may be sinning against him in action. You may be sinning against him in attitude in that your feelings about him may be the blockage. The kind of thing I mean is this: someone may be resentful towards God; in the sort of mood that Job was in. 'God, I don't deserve to suffer like this, you must be wrong, you shouldn't be letting this happen.' There is a spirit of resentment there. And God says do you want to prove that I am wrong so that you can prove that you are in the right? Is that the right attitude to me? Job had not sinned in action, but he certainly did in attitude. God had to deal with that. You can build up a resentment against God because of the way your circumstances have turned out, and you can cease to think of God as a Father and a friend and regard him as a tyrant, even when you pray to him. When you come to God your attitude should be: if an earthly father who is evil knows how to give good gifts to his child, how much more the person I am speaking to wants to give. Am I resentful? Am I bitter toward him? Am I coming with negative feelings into his presence? If so, then no wonder the communication has broken down. God had to deal with Job's attitude and say: Job, should you be thinking about me like this? Should you be trying to prove me in the wrong so that you can be right? Have you forgotten who you are? Job said that he was sorry for having spoken out of turn and out of order.

The other way in which we may have a blockage and not be right with God is in our action: that we are consciously, deliberately continuing to do something of which he does not approve. We are not right with him and the blockage is this: God has called you to fight with him against evil in the world, but the battle has to begin in you, and if you are not even willing to begin the battle in your own life then God sees that you are not on his side, and he will not listen to what you are saying. Therefore if we are treasuring or holding on to that which God has said no to, then we have a hindrance and we cannot get through in prayer.

To people who have said to me, 'I pray and I never get any immediate answers; I never get thoughts coming back to me from my prayer', I have usually said: can I suggest to you a prayer to which you will get an answer within two minutes? It is a prayer that he loves to answer. I say pray this prayer: 'Lord, show me something in my life that you don't like.' Now if you have problems with unanswered prayer, try that one. You will be astonished how quickly he responds, because he wants you right with himself. There, then, is the first hindrance on the earthly side: I am not right with God, either because of my attitude or because of my action. My wrong attitude spoils my feelings towards him; my wrong action spoils his feelings towards me — but either way I am not right with God and I cannot get through.

Now the second blockage is that I am not right with others. This is a very common hindrance to prayer, to getting through. I remember listening to a wonderful Pakistani Christian bishop. He said that one day he was engaged in translating the Bible into Tibetan. He continued — 'I started my work in the study, and I prayed, "Lord, give me fluency, help me to translate the Bible into Tibetan, a language in which the Bible is not yet known."' He got no answer, the heavens were as brass, and he could not get through. He got no inspiration, and he could not get on with the work, and he struggled and struggled and finally, after an hour of struggling, he said, 'Lord, what's the matter?' And the Lord said, 'Why did you shout at your wife this morning for burning the toast at breakfast?' Very simple. He said that as soon as he had gone into the kitchen and put that right, he got through and the translation flowed. That is thoroughly scriptural. Peter, the married apostle, says in his letter, 'You husbands, if you do not treat your wife right, your prayers will not be heard' — never mind answered, they will not even be heard! That is pretty down to earth.

There are two ways in which you can be wrong with people. One is that you do not forgive them for what they have done to you. The only condition in the Lord's Prayer is this: forgive us our trespasses as we forgive — in other words, the forgiveness has to be complete, and your hand must not only hold onto God but your brother's hand too, if forgiveness is to flow. The only thing the Lord's Prayer says you have to do is to forgive those who have hurt you. So important was it that, when Jesus had finished teaching that prayer – which is a shortened version of a Jewish prayer – he then repeated it at the end of the prayer. 'For if you do not forgive, then your Father cannot forgive.' You block the flow. That is quite clear and many know it — but do they do it?

There is another way, however, in which I can have a blockage in my prayer through not being right with others. When they cannot forgive you, that can be a blockage to your prayer. I knew that there is a blockage if I do not forgive them, but I once thought that is all I needed to do and that was all my responsibility. That is what I honestly thought. I went by the text in Romans chapter 12 —*Live peaceably with all men in so far as it in you lies,* and I thought, 'I have got to see that there is nothing in my heart towards them.' However, I read Matthew chapter 5 where it says, *If you are going to worship God, and you remember that your brother has something against you . . .* not: if you remember that you have something against him, go and deal with it. Did you realise that somebody else's attitude to you can be the blockage, whether you are innocent or guilty, whether you hurt consciously or unconsciously — that this can be a blockage to your prayer, not just your attitude to them? So you may need to deal with this. But what if, despite your sincere efforts to restore peacable relations, the other person persists in refusing to forgive you or to accept reconciliation? If, on your part, you have done what you can, God will help you, restore you, and remove the blockage, because his requirement of you here is *in so far as it in you lies*, and his willingness to forgive and restore the repentant person is immeasurably greater and vastly more powerful than the ability of the attitudes of others to hinder your prayer life.

The third issue that can arise on the earthly side of the communication is that I am not right with myself. This is the most extraordinary thing, but again the Lord showed me most clearly a very simple truth: that getting on my knees does not change me. What do I mean by that? I realised that most of the problems people have in their prayer time are problems they have at all other times. That is why they have them, and they are not spiritual problems at all, they are general problems. Let me illustrate. If I was physically exhausted when I was standing up, then my physical exhaustion will affect my prayers when I kneel down. At a point in my life when I was absolutely exhausted for about a week, I had to ask my wife to say my prayers for me every morning, because I was so exhausted – not just in ordinary things – and that carried through into prayer life and I could not pray for myself. Bless her, she prayed for me and read the Bible to me. You cannot suddenly change by getting on your knees.

Or take another aspect. If during the rest of

my life I never concentrate my mind, I just get entertained but never try to educate myself, slip through the headlines, watch the television, never get down to some solid reading on any subject, how can I expect to get down to my Bible study when I start my devotions? I do not suddenly change from being a man whose mind is dissipated, and a man whose mind flits around from one bit of entertainment to another, and become a man who can concentrate in my prayer life.

To take another example, if I am emotionally frustrated in the rest of my life, then I cannot be emotionally at ease in my prayer. It is often true, for example, that some single people are so emotionally frustrated because they are not married that this comes through into their prayer life, and they find that they cannot easily love God because the springs of their affection are all tied up through frustration. But only as they become integrated with their single state, and accept it as a gift from God, and become affectionate within that state, will they find that they can become affectionate in prayer.

So if we are having problems with prayer we

ought perhaps to ask: are these problems general in my life? Am I finding it difficult to concentrate on anything, let alone my Bible? Is my problem in prayer due to what I am outside of my prayer? If I tackle it there, then I can pray. In other words, my life will have an effect on my prayer. If I am culturally stimulated, and if I am physically relaxed, and if I am mentally concentrating in other areas and emotionally integrated in those other areas, then I can come into my prayer life as an integrated, affectionate person.

But it works the other way too — prayer affects the rest of life. If my prayer life is kept in a little watertight compartment, separate from the rest of my life, and I do not pray about the rest of my life, there will be something missing. But if we have identified these problems as life problems rather than simply as spiritual ones, then now I can pray about those life problems.

Are wandering thoughts the problem? The best thing to do with wandering thoughts is to chase them and capture them. Think of a housewife who is trying to have a quiet time after breakfast after her husband has gone off to work. There is all the washing waiting to be done, and her mind keeps thinking about it: whether she will get that stain out — and why do they have to dirty so many shirts? Then other thoughts keep coming in. Now she tries to fight these thoughts and cut them out. It is rather like in the middle of a sermon thinking, 'Did I leave the gas on?' It is so easy. These are wandering thoughts because these are real life. And your wandering thoughts indicate your real concerns. Well then, chase after them, capture them, pray about them, and say, 'Right, Lord, I'll pray about the washing. Instead of feeling guilty that my mind is going to the washing, let me pray about the washing, let me pray about that stain' —and in this way your prayer begins to influence your life, and then your life can influence your prayer. This is getting right with yourself. God accepted you as you were when he justified you, so can you not accept yourself as you are, and let prayer and life be integrated? This is what I mean by getting right with yourself.

Now for the two hindrances that can come on the heavenly side, and can break down communication at that end. I may be right with God, right with others, right with myself, and still find it difficult to get through. So what other causes can there be? Fourth – and this is up in heaven – Satan is fighting you. Notice I have not brought him in until number four. It is far too easy to blame him for the first three, and he is not responsible for many of the things we blame him for. Many of the things that hold us up in our spiritual life are not the devil, but that we are not right with God, right with others or right with ourselves.

But having exhausted those three – and, by the way, do not go on in endless introspection trying to find out which of those three it is – challenge God. Say to him, 'God, I challenge you, if it is one of these three things, then show me; it is up to you to tell me straight away; if you don't tell me straight away, I'll go on to one of the others, so I challenge you to reveal it now.' God loves to answer that kind of an importunate, bold prayer. So do not constantly put the thermometer in your mouth. 'What temperature am I?' When you have said, 'God, I'll go through these three things and will you stop me if I'm not right with you, if I'm not right with someone else, if I'm not right with myself', if he does not stop you, then go on to the fourth and ask: 'Is Satan trying to discourage me?' Satan trembles when he sees the weakest saint upon his knees, and he may be deliberately trying to discourage you from doing that. Do you know that he has at his command legions of evil angels? We call them demons, but that is a misleading word. Are they little black imps running around? No, they are intelligent, supernatural beings, evil angels, and they get in the way of prayer, and do you know that they are highly organised? Do you know that the devil has his foreign office, and that he has an evil angel deliberately assigned to each nation? The Bible makes that quite clear. Therefore, the devil has a foreign ambassador to Britain, an angel whose job it is to disrupt this country.

If you read the book of Daniel you will find all this. And you will find that when Daniel was praying there were two angels fighting over his prayer – one of God's angels and one of Satan's – and Daniel's prayer was not answered for some time until the good angel had beaten the bad angel, and then the answer came through. Your prayer may not be getting through because warfare tends to break lines of communication; it tends to divide, and this spiritual warfare in the heavenly places is going on all the time. Your prayer may just not be getting through the front lines.

Until the battle is won your prayer cannot get through, and so your answer cannot come back. How do you deal with that? You pray about it, and if you feel that Satan is hindering the communications, you pray against Satan in the name of Jesus. You resist him and he runs. Use the blood of Jesus, use the name of Jesus, use every weapon you can from the armoury of Jesus, but fight Satan, resist him. We know that Job got into his problems because Satan was causing them. Now that is the fourth possible hindrance that is causing your prayer to be unanswered, or rather the problem of unacknowledged prayer. You feel that you have sent a letter but it has not been acknowledged.

The final possible hindrance is this: it may be God quite deliberately not replying. Indeed, it is fair to say that if it is Satan it is Satan and God, for Satan can only do something because God allows him — that comes out in the book of Job. Why then would God not reply? Here I want to come to a very positive and a very deep truth, and I do not know if you will be ready to receive it. Why would God not reply when I am right with him, right with others, right with myself and resisting Satan? Shall I tell you? Because he wants you to move up in the school of prayer, and here is a very positive thing to conclude this problem — he is saying: I want you to learn, I want you to make a little extra effort. Have you ever seen a parent teaching a child to walk? At first the parent stays close to the child, then the parent backs up a bit. Why? Because the parent is trying to make the child walk a bit more. Sometimes I believe that God backs up a bit with his saints, saying: try a bit harder, I want you to grow, I want you to mature; plead a bit more. I am going to hold back because I want you to grow in the school of prayer, and I want you to be a strong pray-*er*. The saints will tell you that at the far end of the desert is a promised land of milk and honey.

I believe there are times when God says: Now I have blessed you, now I am not going to reply for a bit because I want you to love me for my own sake, and I want you to seek me, whether you feel I am there or not; I want you to learn.

Now that is a hard and a deep lesson. It is almost like going from primary school to secondary school; you did not like the first few days in a new school, did you? Your roots had been pulled up, your friends had gone, you felt alien, you felt alone. Ah, but you had to move to another school if you were to go on learning and growing. And God wants you to move from the primary to the secondary education in prayer, so he wants you to learn to seek him more. That is the fifth cause, and if you have dealt with the first four and they have all been dismissed from your mind, then say, 'Lord, through you I am going to go on through the dark, through the dry, through the dullness, because I know you are teaching me something very precious.'

* * * * *

We have been thinking about hindrances, but we conclude on an optimistic note: two simple ideas which you must get firmly into your mind if you are going to 'graduate' in the 'school of prayer'.

First: **you can succeed in prayer**. Many people fail because they expect to. They do not think they will succeed. So get this idea firmly in your mind: God the Holy Spirit wants to help you to succeed. So start with this thought: I *can* succeed, I need not be a failure, I can be successful in prayer. The second thought is this: **I will succeed**. Not just I *can* but I *will* — that is, have determination. The Holy Spirit is never going to do your praying for you. Even if you speak in tongues you will do the speaking, you will have to move your lips — he does not do that, as those who have been given the gift find out pretty quickly. The Bible says the Holy Spirit *helps us in our infirmity*; he will help you to do it for yourself, not do it for you. With such an ingenious helper as the Holy Spirit, you can succeed provided you say, 'I will succeed'.

I thank God that one day in glory you will not need any help at all, but you do need help now. Do not approach it by saying, 'I know I'll be a failure; I have had too many failures in the past.' Say, 'Forgetting the things which are behind, I am going to press forward to the things that lie ahead of me, press toward the mark, the goal, the high calling, the prize. I am going to be an athlete in this, and I am going to get to the top and stay there.' And you will find the Holy Spirit will help you all the way; he is the best coach.